Essential
Lille

by Laurence Phillips

Laurence Phillips is a broadcaster and author
of several travel books. A travel and arts
writer specializing in discovering the hidden
corners and little-known treasures of France,
he admits to falling head over heels in love
with Lille. He has presented BBC radio
programmes from the city.

Above: The Grand' Place is Lille's social hub

The 'Ski-Boot' tower dominates the Parc Matisse at Festival time in the new Euralille district

Written by Laurence Phillips

First published 2000
Reprinted Feb, Jun 2001; May 2002; 2003; Feb, Dec 2004.
This edition 2006. Information updated and verified.

© Automobile Association Developments Limited 2003, 2006 . Maps © Automobile Association Developments Limited 2000, 2006

Published by AA Publishing, a trading name of Automobile Association Developments Limited, whose registered office is Fanum House, Basing View, Basingstoke, Hampshire, RG21 4EA. Registered number 1878835.

Automobile Association Developments Limited retains the copyright in the original edition © 2000 and in all subsequent editions, reprints and amendments.

A CIP catalogue record for this book is available from the British Library.

Find out more about AA Publishing and the wide range of services the AA provides by visiting our website at www.theAA.com/bookshop

A02352
Atlas section and cover maps produced from map data supplied by Global Mapping Brackley, UK
© Global Mapping

Colour separation: Keenes, Andover
Printed and bound in Italy by Printer Trento S.r.l.

Contents

About this Book

This book is divided into five sections to cover the most important aspects of your visit to Lille.

Viewing Lille pages 5–10
An introduction to Lille by the author.
The 10 Essentials
The Shaping of Lille
Lille's Features
Lille's Famous

Top Ten pages 11–22
The author's choice of the Top Ten places to see in Lille, listed in alphabetical order, each with practical information.

What to See pages 23–46
The five main areas of Lille and excursions, each with its own brief introduction and an alphabetical listing of the main attractions.
Practical information
Snippets of 'Did you know…' information
2 suggested walks
2 suggested drives
1 feature

Where To... pages 47–58
Detailed listings of the best places to eat, stay, shop, take the children and be entertained.

Practical Matters pages 59–63
A highly visual section containing essential travel information.

Map
All map references are to the map found at the start of the What to See section of this guide.
For example, Palais des Beaux-Arts has the reference ✚ 25D2—indicating the page on which the map is located and the grid square in which the museum is to be found. The map used in this travel guide is included in the index.

Prices
Where appropriate, an indication of the cost of an establishment is given by € signs:
€€€ denotes higher prices, €€ denotes average prices, while € denotes lower charges.

Star Ratings
Most of the places described in this book have been given a separate rating:
✪✪✪　　Do not miss
✪✪　　　Highly recommended
✪　　　　Worth seeing

Viewing
Lille

Above: *Celebrated fish restaurant, l'Huitrière*
Right: *The 43ème RI at the Citadelle garrison*

Laurence Phillips' Lille

Art Underground
Many métro stations are home to gems from Lille's modern art collection. At Porte de Valenciennes, the massive human hand created by César appears to carry the entire station. Enjoy the unexpected image of a barge loaded with flour at the Porte des Postes and the bas-relief of old ladies crossing a railway line at Rihour.

Lille is a city with a talent for making new friends. It's more than the world-class museums, national theatre, ballet company and internationally renowned orchestra. More than the serious shopping, from Cartier to the flea market, the good food, great beers, cider and locally distilled *genièvre*. What keeps the atmosphere bubbling is the people; the warmest and most genuinely welcoming in France. It was deservedly chosen as the European Capital of Culture for 2004.

I remember getting hopelessly lost once, in the warren of cobbles and gables that is the old town. I asked a stranger for directions and was courteously escorted to my destination. Every turn is the entrance to another side of town. Step into the place du Général de Gaulle and arrive at a party. In the Bois de Boulogne, jog around the majestic Citadelle and find Louis XIV's chosen route into the town he considered his favourite conquest. Tread the evening streets of Vieux Lille and find the keys to its history.

Lille works her magic whatever the season and whatever the weather; from the morning in spring when the city awakens to find its pavements and squares carpeted in a thousand blooms, to the rain glistening on polished cobbles, the glint of sunlight on the gilded roofs of the Grand' Place and the alchemy that turns the grey skies of winter into breathtaking illuminations for the basement galleries of the Palais des Beaux-Arts.

But the real magic in a city so rich in history and brimful of tomorrow's possibilities is that you always leave Lille feeling just a little bit younger than when you arrived.

Huge pans of paella and couscous to feed the thousands at Wazemmes Sunday market

THE **10** ESSENTIALS

If you only have a short time to visit Lille, here are ten essentials which together create a portrait of the city:

• **See everything in one hour** on the multilingual mini-bus tour that leaves the Palais Rihour Tourist Office on the hour.
☎ 03 59 57 94 00.

• **Get lost in the old town** and find little shops and galleries, best discovered on foot (➤ 21).

• **Raise a glass of the local beer.** In bottles try Les 3 Monts, Ch'ti or La Goudale, or order a *palette de degustation* (tasting tray) at Les Brasseurs, the station brasserie which brews everything in house (➤ 50).

• **Ride the métro** – the world's first fully automated driverless subway system. Keep going in one direction by métro, tram and bus all on one ticket.

• **Window shop for your next meal** as you check out the eateries along the rue de Gand (➤ 48).

• **Hang around the Grand' Place,** with a coffee, magazine or shopping list, and just watch the world go by (➤ 18).

• **Spend time wallowing in beauty** at the Palais des Beaux-Arts. The galleries are a cultural haven in a lively city (➤ 17).

• **Enter the scrum for bargains** at Wazemmes food and flea market on a Sunday morning (➤ 22).

• **Join the shopping throng** in the pedestrian streets around rue de Béthune.

• **Take time** to admire some classic art deco architecture above many of the shop fronts and cinema entrances.

• **Pause for a breath of fresh air** in the Bois de Boulogne or the Jardin Vauban (➤ 12 and 28).

Right: *A Grand' Place table is the best place to watch the city go by*

Below: *Bric-à-brac takes to the streets at the annual Braderie and weekend markets*

Above: *The Jardin Vauban, designed for strolling*

The Shaping of Lille

1066
L'Isle mentioned in charter, describing charitable donation by Baudoin V, Count of Flanders. He owned a stronghold on the site of today's cathedral. Charter describes a forum where the Grand' Place now stands.

1205
Crusades. Count Baudoin IX crowned Emperor of Constantinople. His daughters are raised by King Philippe Auguste of France. Eldest daughter Jeanne marries Ferrand of Portugal and comes to live in Lille.

1214
Flanders unites with Holy Roman Emperor Otto IV and King John of England against France, but loses Battle of Bouvines. King Philippe Auguste takes Lille, which he gives to Jeanne.

1369
Lille joins Burgundian Empire when Marguerite of Flanders marries Philippe Le Temoine.

1453
Philippe le Bon builds Palais Rihour and holds court in Lille.

1477
Marie de Bourgogne marries Maximillian of Austria. Lille passes to the Hapsburgs. When Charles V of Spain becomes Emperor, Lille and the Netherlands become Spanish.

1663
Maria-Theresa of Spain marries Louis XIV of France, who claims his wife's heritage in the Low Countries.

1667
Louis XIV of France captures Lille. Commissions Vauban to build Citadelle. Town enlarged with strict building regulations.

1708–13
War of Spanish Succession. Lille occupied by the Dutch.

1792
Lille defies a seige by an army of 35,000 Austrians.

1846
First Paris–Lille railway line completed.

1854–57
Louis Pasteur becomes first Dean of the Faculty of Science (▶ 10).

1890
Birth of Charles de Gaulle (▶ 10).

1914
German troops take Lille after three days of resistance; 900 houses destroyed.

1940
Lille holds out against the German invasion for three days. Rommel seizes the town 1 June.

1966
Creation of the Communauté Urbaine embracing nearby towns.

1981–84
Lille's mayor, Pierre Mauroy, becomes President Mitterrand's first Prime Minister.

1983
Inauguration of world's first fully automated transport system.

1993
High-speed TGV link means Paris is now only one hour away.

1994
Launch of Channel Tunnel, Eurostar TGV-Nord Link uniting Paris, Brussels, London and Lille. Inauguration of Euralille.

1997
Reopening of Palais des Beaux-Arts as France's second national art collection.

1999
Cathedral Notre Dame de la Treille completed.

2004
Lille is European Capital of Culture.

Lille's Features

Lille's name is a corruption of the word 'l'île', the island (Rijsel in Flemish), because when the town was founded it was little more than a village surrounded by waterways. As the town grew, the tributaries of the River Deûle were channelled into canals and a trading port.

Since Lille lies on chalky soil just 20m (65ft) above sea level, 11th-century merchants from Bruges and Ghent travelling to the prosperous fairs of Champagne were unable to navigate the Upper Deûle, and they were obliged to take their goods by cart to the port of the town 1km (0.5 miles) away. And so a market town was born.

Today's city has a population of 220,000, but the wider urban area is home ot 1,100,000. Some 10 per cent of the population is comprised of students at engineering, business, arts and journalism faculties in Lille and Villeneuve d'Ascq.

As the local tourist literature states proudly, Lille was once the capital of Flanders, and is now the capital of Nord-Pas de Calais, France's second region. The new urban area of 87 communes, a genuinely international district, sprawls over 879km (545 miles) and extends into Belgium.

Lille's youngest: 28 per cent of the city's population is under 20.

Lille's most legitimate: more legal eagles per head than anywhere else in France: 12,300 law students, 600 lawyers and 44 court bailiffs and 6 major international law firms.

Lille's biggest: home to Europe's biggest bookshop, with half a million books in stock, 8,000sq m (86,000sq ft) floorspace on eight floors, linked by footbridges.

Lille's newest: the 19th-century cathedral was completed in 1999.

Lille's best dressed: Lille is Europe's mail order capital and the biggest textile trading area in France.

Economy

France's fourth largest city (after Paris, Lyon and Marseille) and its second for insurance companies, printing and publishing. It is the nation's third financial centre, with 600 banks and scores of credit companies and stock brokerages. Lille is the third river port, the third largest chemical, health and pharmaceutical research centre, and the third largest industrial zone.

Eurostar and the new Gare Lille-Europe brought a new era to the city

Lille's Famous

Louis Pasteur (1822–95)

The legendary microbiologist discovered that germs cause disease, and subsequently created vaccines for rabies, cholera and anthrax, as well as giving his name to pasteurisation. He came to Lille in 1863 as Dean of the new university's Faculté des Sciences, pioneered evening classes for workers, and established the Institute Pasteur. His laboratory research into fermentation revolutionized wine making and brewing.

Louis Pasteur

Braderie de Lille
One of Lille's biggest attractions is not a person or a building, but an event—Europe's biggest flea market, the Braderie, which takes place every September (► 58).

Charles de Gaulle (1890–1970)

War hero and first president of the Fifth Republic (1958–69), de Gaulle was born in the rue Princesse. Graduating from St. Cyr military academy and wounded in World War I, he refused to accept Marshal Pétain's truce with Germany in 1940 and rallied Free French troops with his historic broadcast from London on 18 June 1940. In 1944 he returned to Paris in triumph and headed the provisional government. He created the present presidential system, oversaw the independence of Algeria, famously opposed British influence in Europe, withdrew France from NATO in 1966 and crushed student uprisings in May 1968.

Charles d'Artagnan

Charles de Batz de Castelmore, Comte d'Artagnan, hero of Dumas' *Three Musketeers*, was in real life the second governor of Lille. His 1672 home in rue de la Grande Chaussée is now a shoe shop. D'Artagnan died at the siege of Maastricht in 1673.

Pierre Mauroy (1928–)

Senator and mayor of Lille (1973–2001) and first socialist Prime Minister of the Fifth Republic (1981–84), Pierre Mauroy campaigned for the Channel Tunnel link to pass through Lille between Paris, London and Brussels. His vision of Lille's renaissance led to the creation of Euralille and the city's new international role.

Top Ten

Above: *Classic maritime mosaics adorn the outside of L'Huitrière restaurant*
Right: *Traditional signs in the oldest street in town*

RUE de la MONNAIE

1
Bois de Boulogne

🕂 24A4, 24A5

🕓 Daily

🚌 14 Jardin Vauban

↔ Citadelle (▶ 13), Jardin Vauban (▶ 29)

❓ Funfairs during French school holidays

Zoo

✉ avenue Mathias Delobel

☎ 03 28 52 07 00

🕓 Summer Mon–Fri 9–5.30, Sat, Sun 9–6.30; winter daily 10–5. Closed 2nd Sun Dec–2nd Sun Feb

🖐 Free

❓ Guided visits by appointment

The Deûle wraps itself around the Bois and the Citadelle

Surrounded by water, this is the biggest green space in town, and everyone's favourite Sunday afternoon walk.

Fifty hectares (124 acres) of countryside within the city limits are home to panthers, soldiers and fitness fanatics. The Bois de Boulogne envelopes the Citadelle (▶ 13), and is itself wrapped in the loop of the canal of the River Deûle, with its picturesque lock gates of the Ecluse de la Barre. The park begins with the tree-lined Esplanade, first planted by Vauban in 1675, then crosses the canal at the Pont de Ramponneau to the Champs de Mars, home to school holiday funfairs. A cobbled track leading to the fortress is popular with cyclists toughening up for the notorious Paris-Roubaix street-cycling race. This is held every April and is known to riders as 'The Hell of The North'. Sunday morning is the joggers' rush hour. Look out for the French soldiers and Foreign Legionnaires in their blue tracksuits, and the more fashionably attired townsfolk and visitors following a signposted exercise circuit around the fortifications, between the willow trees and beneath the drawbridges. The former moat, now grassed over, was where occupying forces executed members of the French Resistance movements during the two world wars. A memorial to the victims, Félix Desruelle's Monument aux Fusillées, stands just outside the Bois at the Square Daubenton. The park is also home to the **town zoo**. Lille's panthers, zebras and rhinos welcome visitors, as do the residents of Iles aux Singes (Monkey Islands). At the entrance to the animal park is a children's playground with dodgems, rides and candyfloss stalls.

2
Citadelle

The magnificent pentagonal star–shaped fortress surrounded by trees has been the hub of the French army for 300 years.

24A4, 24A5

avenue du 42ème Régiment d'Infantrie

Office de Tourisme 03 20 21 94 21

The Tourist Office can organize guided visits during holiday periods. 08 91 56 20 04. Advance reservation essential. Meet at the Porte Royale

14 Jardin Vauban

Good but streets are cobbled

Moderate

Bois de Boulogne (► 12), Jardin Vauban (► 29)

Louis XIV commissioned the great military architect Vauban to build his 'Queen of Citadelles' outside Vieux Lille. Constructed in record time between 1667 and 1670, the Citadelle used 16 million bricks. Massive ramparts, banked with soil to absorb the impact of artillery fire, bear witness to the genius of the engineer who fortified northern France. A town in its own right, with five bastions, one at each point of the star, and five half-moon fortifications, the classic design inspired the US Pentagon. The main entrance is the Porte Royale, an important strategic and morale-boosting symbol of the monarchy and France itself. It has a Latin-inscribed regal façade, walls 4m (4.4yds) thick and stands at an angle to the drawbridge to evade enemy fire. Designed for 1,200, the garrison remains home to 1,000 soldiers who wear naval badges since the first regiment stationed here was a marine troop. A ship's mast stands in the central parade ground. The King was a regular guest and he later commissioned a new residential *quartier royale* between the Citadelle and Vieux Lille. The architect was rewarded with the title Governor of the Citadelle. His successor was d'Artagnan (► 10) and vestiges of their private entrance to the chapel may still be seen with the renovated arsenal and officers quarters.

Twenty-eight similar citadels made a double row of border defences from the North Sea to the Ardennes. Many are open to the public on the fourth Sunday in April. Vauban's original models of the fortified towns are displayed at the Palais des Beaux-Arts (► 17).

Above: *The Porte Royale is as much a monument to the power of the Sun King (Louis XIV) as a key defensive gate*

3
Euralille

Consumerism by night—Euralille's massive shopping mall

The modern shopping and leisure district straddles the new TGV and Eurostar station.

✚ 25F4

✉ Euralille, avenue Le Courbusier

☎ (Euralille) 03 20 14 52 20, (Carrefour hypermarket) 03 20 15 56 00, (Aeronef) 03 28 38 50 50

🕐 Mon–Sat 10–8; hypermarket 9am–10pm; restaurants 10am–midnight

🍴 Various cafés-restaurants (€–€€) on site

Ⓢ Gare Lille-Europe

🚌 All buses and trams

🚆 Lille-Europe, Lille-Flandres

♿ Excellent

↔ Porte de Roubaix (► 36)

This city of tomorrow is a huge monument to the optimism of Lille and its leaders. From Christian de Portzampac's Tour Credit Lyonnais, known locally as the 'Ski-Boot', perched above the glass and chrome Gare Europe, to the dramatic Centre Euralille shopping mall, this huge business and leisure development is the key to the city's renaissance. Designed to serve more than 10 times the population of Lille, here you can shop for essentials or luxuries, attend some of Europe's most talked-about parties, enjoy concerts, or even prepare a meal in a rented apartment. Opened with the Channel Tunnel in 1994, Rem Koolhaas's futurescape sprawls across 70ha (173 acres) of city-centre land formerly owned by the army. In other historic cities such modernism might jar, but this quarter sits very comfortably alongside the 19th-century Gare Lille-Flandres, and across the newly landscaped Parc Matisse from the old city gate Porte de Roubaix (► 36). At street level there are 140 shops, a hypermarket, holiday apartments and a hotel. Below lies the Parvis François Mitterand—rollerbladers' heaven. High above the streets in one of the tower blocks is Aeronef, the once unofficial nightclub and music venue. Across the way, and alongside the périphérique ring road, is Koolhaas's own architectural contribution to the project. The massive oval Grand Palais is both a conference centre and 5,000-seat concert arena.

4
Musée d'Art Moderne
(Museum of Modern Art)

The gardens and galleries of the museum of modern art are home to 20th-century masterpieces and works by contemporary artists.

It's just seven minutes by métro from central Lille to the town of Villeneuve d'Ascq (➤ 41) then a six-minute bus ride to the gates of a park where dog walkers and local families take the air. Large sculptures are dotted amongst the trees and gardens. Picasso's *Femme aux Bras Ecartés* and Alexander Calder's *Southern Cross* stride the lavish lawns surrounding Roland Simounet's brick building, which was built in 1983 to house the collections donated to the community by Roger Dutilleul and Jean and Geneviève Masurel. The light, airy galleries begin with a room devoted to Modigliani's *Nu Assis à la Chemise* and *Maternité*. The collection is comprehensive, from the Rouaults and Derains of the Fauvist room to a Cubism hall displaying Braque's *Maison et Arbres* and *Sacre Coeur Montmartre*, six Picassos, including his *Musical Instruments* and *Death Head* and works by Henri Laurens. The Surrealist department includes paintings by Miro and Masson. The permanent collection has excellent examples of the Paris, Montparnasse and Art Naif schools. Large, full-length windows between the showrooms offer glimpses of the garden displays in the sunlight. In addition to the original donation of French work from the first half of the century, the museum has acquired an enviable range of work by contemporary artists, among them Eduardo Arroyo, Richard Deacon, François Dufrène and Dennis Oppenheim. A schedule of temporary exhibitions features installation art and challenging, sometimes controversial, thematic shows by today's artists. The museum shop sells original and unusual jewellery by local artists.

✚ 25F3

✉ 1 allée du Musée, Villeneuve d'Ascq

☎ 03 20 19 68 68.

🕐 Due to close late 2005 for renovations. Phone for details of temporary exhibions in the area.

🍽 Café-Restaurant (€)

Ⓜ Pont de Bois, then 🚌 41 to Parc Urbain-Musée

♿ Excellent

✋ Moderate, free entry 1st Sun each month

Below: *Modigliani's* Nu Assis à la Chemise *(1917)*
Bottom: *The garden*

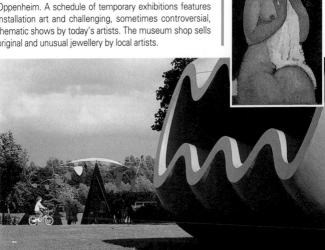

5
Musée de l'Hospice Comtesse

🕂 25D5

✉ 32 rue de la Monnaie

☎ 03 28 36 84 00

🕔 Mon 2–6, Wed–Sun 10–12.30 and 2–6. Closed Tue, 1 Jan, 1 May, 14 Jul, 1 Nov, 25 Dec and Braderie weekend.

🍴 Many restaurants and cafes near by (€–€€€)

🚌 3,6,9 Lion d'Or

♿ Very limited access to cobbled courtyard and chapel only

✋ Cheap, free for children under 12. Free entry 1st Sun each month

↔ Vieux Lille (➤ 21), Old Town Walk (➤ 38)

❓ Guided tour available most afternoons at no extra charge. Occasional weekend concerts

Traditional blue and white tiling of old Flanders

The 13th-century hospital provides a charming glimpse of Lille's life and art from the 15th to the 17th centuries.

Hidden behind the old shopfronts of the rue de la Monnaie, the Musée de l'Hospice Comtesse is a model of discretion. Founded as a hospital by Jeanne de Constantinople, Countess of Flanders, in 1237, the museum has preserved many of Lille's past lives. The restored 15th-century hospital ward, with maritime timber vaultings, and the 17th-century chapel and convent, retaining traces of the original murals, often host musical recitals. Much of the museum is devoted to salvaged images of Lille and the Low Countries through the ages. The kitchen is decorated in Dutch-influenced blue and white tiling. Wooden panels in the parlour are illuminated with 17th-century portraits of local children. The collection of northern French, Dutch and Flemish paintings, including works by Watteau, is complemented by examples of furniture making and wood carving from the periods. Not to be missed are the tapestries of Guillaume Werniers, the weaver of old Lille. The museum also houses a collection of rare, ancient musical instruments. Not simply a museum, the Hospice Comtesse is the custodian of the very spirit of Lille. The legendary generosity and sense of community that has marked out the city over the centuries, through times of wealth and poverty, was born here in the hospital and chapel. Lille has pioneered mass education, childcare and welfare, and the concept of looking after the needy was the *raison d'être* of the Countess's hospice and chapel. The stillness and intimacy of the oldest buildings around the courtyard provide a contemplative haven for many visitors today.

6

Palais des Beaux-Arts
(Fine Arts Museum)

France's second national museum after the Louvre, built 1889–92, was reopened by President Chirac in 1997 after six years of renovation.

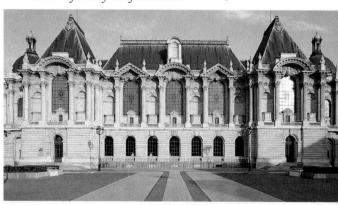

Climb the magnificent staircases to the first floor, taking time to admire the stained-glass windows illustrating arts and crafts. No one should miss the museum's celebrated Goyas, a pair of wicked portrayals of youth and old age (*Les Vieilles* and *Les Jeunes*). In side galleries, deep red walls and high ceilings provide the perfect backdrop to a veritable banquet of French, Flemish and European masterpieces from the 17th to the 19th centuries, including Rubens Descente de Croix and works of Van Dyck, Corot, Delacroix and the collection's first curator Wattau. A superb gallery devoted to the impressionists includes treasures by Monet, Van Gogh, Renoir and Sisley, as well as Lautrec and individual casts of Rodin's *Burghers of Calais*. A special hall on the ground floor takes in 100 years of French sculpture by the leading figures of the 19th century. The remarkable basement attractions should not be missed: Donatello's bas relief *Festin d'Herod*, and 40 Raphaël sketches, the highlights of the Renaissance and Medieval collection. Another hall houses major temporary exhibitions under natural light, the glass ceiling part of a remarkable prism deflecting sunshine via the glazed wall of the museum's administrative block. The final chamber is a walk through the fortified cities of northern France. There are Vauban's original models of his citadel and garrison towns from Calais to the Ardennes (▶ 13). The light, airy atrium and terrace are free, open to all, and an ideal place to break for a coffee or browse the museum shop.

✚ 25D2

✉ place de la République

☎ 03 20 06 78 00, guided tours 03 20 06 78 17

🕐 Mon 2–6; Wed–Thu, Sat–Sun 10–6; Fri 10–7. Closed public holidays

🍴 Good café and restaurant (€) with terrace on site

Ⓜ République

♿ Excellent

✋ Moderate, free access to atrium. Free entry to museum 1st Sun each month

❓ Bookshop and gift shop

↔ Walk (▶ 34–35)

Above: *The Palais des Beaux-Arts is home to 400 years of European masterpieces*

17

7

Les Places

✚ 25D3

🍴 Dozens of restaurants and cafés (€–€€)

🚇 Rihour

🛈 place Rihour

♿ Good

✋ Free

↔ Vieille Bourse (➤ 20), Vieux Lille (➤ 21), Old Town Walk (➤ 38)

The Grand' Place (known to maps and postmen as the place du Général de Gaulle) and its two neighbours are the physical and spiritual heart of Lille.

The partly pedestrian-only place de Gaulle constantly reinvents itself. One week a landscaped garden, the next a ploughed farmyard, or perhaps a fairytale Christmas grotto with a gigantic ferris wheel. At midnight in January relish the rooftop and clocktower panorama from a swaying cradle high above the cobbles. Everyone's rendezvous is the central fountain around the statue of the Déesse—a goddess and spiritual symbol of civic courage during the 1792 siege. Gossips note her physical resemblance to the wife of the mayor who commissioned the monument from the artist Benvignat. The Théâtre du Nord (➤ 57) graces the stepped, galleried façade of the former Grand' Garde, the King's guardhouse. The neighbouring tiered roof, topped with golden figures, is the 1936 home of the local

Rendezvous central, the main meeting points are the place de Gaulle and the restaurants between the squares (inset)

paper *La Voix du Nord*. It dominates the square along with the Furet du Nord, Europe's largest bookshop with half a million volumes over eight storeys. Place de Gaulle trickles into place Rihour, home of the Palais Rihour (► 33) and tourist office. The squares are linked by a seamless run of restaurants, cafés and bars where late night revellers adjourn for onion soup breakfast in the small hours. Across the place de Gaulle, behind the Vieille Bourse (► 20) is the place du Théâtre. Here see the neoclassical Opera House, with its monumental sculptures of Apollo and the Muses, and the magnificent belfry of the imposing Chambre de Commerce et d'Industrie – both built in the 1920s by Louis Cordonnier.

Below: *The Opera House was restored to its former glory in 2004*

Opposite is the Rang de Beauregard, an exquisitely finished 1687 terrace of 14 houses and shops designed to complement the Vieille Bourse.

8
Vieille Bourse

The ornate 17th-century merchant exchange building remains an elegant civilized sanctuary where culture meets commerce in style.

Undeniably the most beautiful building in Lille, the Vieille Bourse, standing between the places du Théâtre and de Gaulle, is an opulent masterpiece of the Flemish renaissance. Created in 1652–53 to house the Bourse de Commerce, or trading exchange, it comprises 24 identical houses built around a courtyard. The exquisite decoration owes its flamboyance to the fact that the builder, Julien Destrez, was a noted carpenter and sculptor of wood. Thus exuberant garlands and masks flourish on the outer walls, and lush fruits and flowers ornament the courtyard in the style of fine Flemish furnishings. Sculpted Lions of Flanders guard each of the four entrances to the court.

The cloisters of commerce inside the Vieille Bourse

Today's visitors may notice a second row of emblems and arms below the second storey windows. These are logos of 20th century businesses that funded the restoration of the Vieille Bourse to its former glory. The merchants' stalls within the cloister are now marked with plaques, medallions and busts honouring Lille's great men of science and letters. Although the original business practices outgrew their early home, leading to the construction of the Chambre de Commerce et d'Industrie in 1921, the Vieille Bourse continues trading as a second-hand book market. A quiet meeting place for the contemplative, there is always at least one game of chess in progress in the northeastern corner of the courtyard. On Sundays in July and August the building takes on yet another identity, as Belgian, Dutch and French lovers of tangos, java and waltzes join the afternoon tea-dance.

9
Vieux Lille

The winding, cobbled streets, with names evoking hunchbacked cats and golden lions, are home to enchanting shops selling linens and antiques.

Maps never quite capture the confusing reality of this most serpentine of districts, as the complex knot of narrow tributaries of the rues Royale, de la Monnaie and Basse defy the concepts of right angles and parallel lines. This means that your destination is never quite where you expect it to be. So be prepared to stumble on Notre Dame de la Treille (► 32), the Musée de l'Hospice Comtesse (► 16) or the art deco façade of fish shop and gastronomic dining room l'Huîtrière (► 49) more than once in an afternoon. The buildings, constructed from Armentières brick and Lezennes white stone, have beautifully sculpted cherubs, wheatsheaves and horns of plenty above the arched doorways. The vibrant hues and striking exposed beams of the 17th-century shopping streets have been lovingly restored since the district was reclaimed from decay in the 1960s. The oldest street is the rue de la Monnaie, once the mint. The most impressive house is the baroque Demeure Gilles de la Boë (1636), 29 place Louise de Bettignies, that once overlooked the inland port, built over in the 18th century. Fanning out from the place du Lion d'Or are countless craft shops, boutiques and *estaminet* bars. Antique dealers and jewellers jostle alongside couturiers and wine merchants from place du Concert to the Grand' Place archway of the rue des débris St Etienne. The rue de Gand's cobbles, leading to the fortified Porte de Gand (► 36), pass dozens of intimate restaurants.

24C5

Many restaurants and cafés near by (€–€€€)

3, 6, 9 Lion d'Or

Hospice Comtesse (► 16), Old Town Walk (► 38)

Guided tour details from tourist office

Tall, narrow 17th-century houses in the old town

10
Wazemmes

📍 24B1

✉ place de la Nouvelle Aventure

🕐 Sun, Tue and Thu 7–2

🍴 Many bars, cafes and food stalls nearby (€)

🚇 Gambetta

♿ Good, but crowded

Food market, clothes market, antiques market, and a street–party every weekend: the Sunday morning Marché de Wazemmes is the stuff of legend.

More than a mere market, this is an occasion. Never mind the Braderie (▶ 58), the spirit of Wazemmes spills out into the streets every Sunday morning. As rue Gambetta escapes from place de la République and approaches the marketplace, little shops and bigger stores fling open their doors to welcome the thousands making the pilgrimage to this bustling multicultural hub of Lille's weekend. From Gambetta métro station, pause to simper over the puppies, kittens, bunnies and chickens of the pet market, then follow the surging crowd towards the streets around the Church of St. Paul et St. Pierre. Here haggle over antiques, bric-à-brac, second-hand crockery, fireplaces and paperbacks. On the place de la Nouvelle Aventure are toy-sellers, clothes rails, knitwear tables, and the market gardeners' fruit and vegetable stalls piled with plump fresh chicory, huge hearted celeriac and rosy radishes. For meats, fish and cheeses, the brick-built market hall at the end of the square is a sensory delight. Nonetheless, the true carnival atmosphere belongs to the streets outside, where the sounds of an accordion from an outdoor café mingle with the spiel of traders selling saucepans from an open-backed truck or bunches of fresh mint from panniers strapped to an old bicycle. All is handshakes, backslapping and bonhomie. The aroma of Sunday lunch is over-whelming. Huge pans of paella and couscous are stirred outside the many ethnic restaurants, and giant rotisseries turn dozens of roast chickens, their juices basting trays of baby roast potatoes beneath. The best way to appreciate this cacophony is to surrender to its flow.

Find flowers by the rue Gambetta and (right) crockery in the rue St-Pierre St-Paul

What to See

Above: *Reflections of the Palais des Beaux-Arts*
Right: *A grateful mother offers her child to Louis Pasteur in his extravagant memorial on the place Lebon*

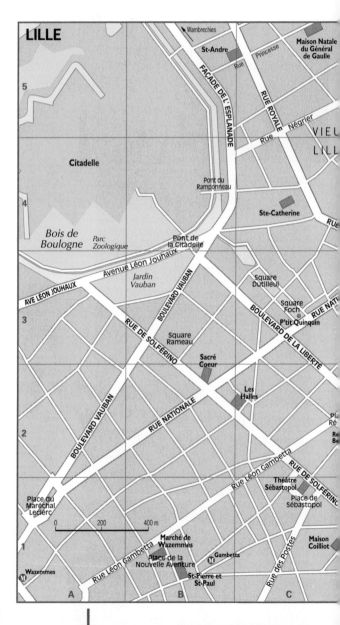

LILLE

Wambrechies

St-Andre

Maison Natale
du Général
de Gaulle

Rue Princesse

RUE ROYALE

Rue Négrier

FAÇADE DE L'ESPLANADE

VIEL

LILL

Citadelle

Pont du
Ramponneau

Ste-Catherine

RUE

Bois de
Boulogne

Parc
Zoologique

Pont de
la Citadelle

Avenue Léon Jouhaux

AVE LÉON JOUHAUX

Jardin
Vauban

BOULEVARD VAUBAN

square
Dutilleul

Square
Foch

RUE NATI

BOULEVARD DE LA LIBERTÉ

P'tit Quinquin

RUE DE SOLFERINO

Square
Rameau

Sacré
Cœur

Les
Halles

Pl
Ré

Re
Be

BOULEVARD VAUBAN

RUE NATIONALE

Rue Léon Gambetta

RUE DE SOLFERIN

Théâtre
Sébastopol

Place de
Sébastopol

Place du
Maréchal
Leclerc

0   200   400 m

Marché de
Wazemmes

Rue Léon Gambetta

Maison
Coilliot

Place de la
Nouvelle Aventure

Gambetta

Rue des Postes

Wazemmes

St-Pierre et
St-Paul

A   B   C

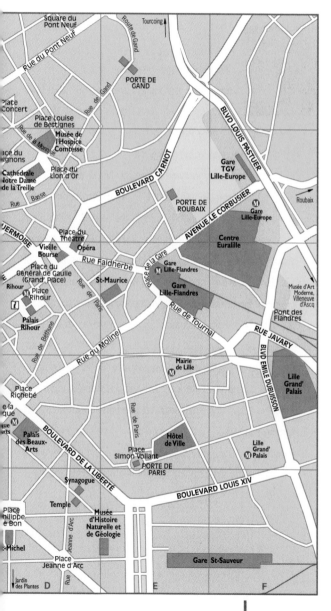

Lille

Lille's advantage over other major cities is that most of its attractions are a comfortable walk away. Its history, and Spanish, Dutch, Flemish, Burgundian and finally French heritage, guarantees plenty of distractions en route from one sight to the next.

Each quarter has its individual identity. North of the Grand' Place is the perfectly preserved 17th- and 18th-century town. Around place de la République, find the legacy of the great 19th-century benefactors of the city. Early 20th-century themes characterize the central shopping area, and the cityscapes of the new era are heralded by the wide spaces and soaring towers of the Euralille district. Around the edges of the city are reminders of the glorious past of a great military town.

Because each chapter in Lille's story was carefully planned, every generation has offered its people fresh open spaces in which to take the air. The Bois de Boulogne was the gift of the Sun King, Louis XIV. The Jardin Vauban dates from the age of learning and reason when Lille became a university town in the 19th century. The Parc Matisse saw in the 21st century and a new Parc Lebas emerged by the old freight station in 2005.

> *'This is the Paris of the Low Countries'*
>
> Anonymous 18th-century traveller

Exploring Lille

Since modern Lille expanded into a metropolitan area, the best way to enjoy its full potential is with the excellent public transport system, spreading across the border into Belgium. Almost any destination may be reached by métro, tram or bus.

City Pass
1-day €20, 2-day €30, 3-day €45

One ticket allows travel in any one direction, no matter how many changes. Tickets can be purchased individually, in a carnet of ten, or as an inexpensive day pass, and must be punched at the start of every journey. You can buy them on board but it's cheaper to buy in advance. The Lille Métropole City Pass, from the tourist office, offers unlimited use of public transport and entry to museums as well as discounts at concerts.

The métro is the fastest, but there are no stations in the old part of town. Buses serve the harder-to-reach areas, and each stop has a name, is clearly marked on the map from stations and tourist offices, and displays a printed timetable.The leisurely route to Roubaix and Tourcoing is the tramway. Gliding through wide thoroughfares of leafy suburbs with excellent views of the Addams Family-style perpendicular houses and manicured parks of the dormitory towns.

The independent hire bicycles, while the unhurried sightseer just strolls through the city. It is impossible to do everything in one visit—and there is always the next time.

> ## DID YOU KNOW?
>
> The city at your feet: Lisle stockings and socks get their name from Lille, where the smooth, tightly twisted threads of long-staple cotton were first sold.

A vintage tram brings hints of the past to the new campus town of Villeneuve d'Ascq

What to See in Lille

BEFROI DE L'HOTEL DE VILLE (TOWN HALL BELFRY) ✪

➕ 25E2
✉ place Roger Salengro
☎ 03 20 49 50 00
🕐 Check with tourist office for limited opening hours
🚇 Mairie de Lille
♿ Few. Partial access to town hall, but over 100 steps to Belfry
💶 Free Mon–Fri, cheap Sun, public holidays
↔ Porte de Paris (► 36)

The 104m (341ft) bell tower of the Hotel de Ville is supported by Lille's two sculpted giants Lydéric and Phinaert, legendary founders of the city. Take the steps and a lift to the top to take advantage of an exellent photo opportunity. Opened in 1932, it was the crowning glory of the new town hall replacing the original in place Rihour, destroyed by fire in 1916. Emille Dubuisson's ferro-concrete creation was inspired by traditional gabled Flemish architecture. The impressive central hall is over 100m (109yds) long and studded with floral pillars. The story of the town is told in a strip cartoon fresco by the Icelandic painter Erro, and the building hosts contemporary art shows.

BOIS DE BOULOGNE (► 12, TOP TEN)

CITADELLE (► 13, TOP TEN)

EURALILLE (► 14, TOP TEN)

The belfry at the heart of the former St-Saveur district where the Internationale *was first sung*

Hector's House, Guimard's Parisian flamboyance in a quiet residential street

JARDIN VAUBAN ⭐⭐

Almost an overflow from the Bois de Boulogne across the canal, this delightful park was designed in 1865 by Barillet Deschamps, then the Head Gardener of Paris. Romantic and enchanting paths twist and turn past neat lawns, waterfalls, a grotto and various memorials to writers and musicians. Monsieur Rameau's Goat House is a charming outdoor **marionette theatre** in the summer months. A tiny, tidy orchard is the place to go for helpful advice on fruit growing and tutored pruning sessions. By the square Daubenton is a monument to local hero Charles de Gaulle (► 10 and 32).

🕂 24B3
✉ Boulevard Vauban
🕐 Daily
🚇 14 Jardin Vauban
♿ Very good
↔ Bois de Boulogne (► 12), Citadelle (► 13)

Marionette Theatre
☎ 03 20 42 09 95
🕐 Wed pm Apr–Sep

MAISON COILLIOT ⭐

Curiosity is its own reward and although private, nosiness is expected of anyone passing this terraced house in a residential street. Monsieur Coilliot, a ceramics maker, commissioned Hector Guimard to design his home. Guimard was the art nouveau architect of the Paris Métro, and his trademark green swirls, enamel lettering and flamboyant whiplashes soon established the Maison Coilliot as the most remarkable house in town. Everyone is tempted to peer through the windows and look up at the fantasy balconies and double gables of a building designed for prying eyes.

🕂 24C1
✉ 14 rue Fleurus
🚇 14 Lebon
↔ Palais des Beaux-Arts (► 17), Walk (► 34–35)

DID YOU KNOW?

The will of eccentric horticulturist Charles Rameau, whose legacy to the town includes the Palais Rameau (► 35) and the Jardin Vauban Goat House (► above), decrees that his grave must always be marked with a vine, potatoes, a tomato plant, rose bush, dahlias and a strawberry bed. This unusual memorial may be seen at the Cimetière du Sud.

In the Know

If you only have a short time to visit Lille and would like to get a real flavour of the city, here are some ideas:

10

Ways To Be a Local

Be seen with *Sortir,* the free listings magazine on a Wednesday and *La Voix du Nord* at all other times, when sitting at a pavement café.

Order beer instead of wine with your lunch.

Lunch outdoors on the Grand' Place.

Dine around Les Halles on a Friday or Saturday but choose the rue de Gand for *diner à deux*.

Order onion soup at dawn at Le Chicorée after a night on the town.

Meet your friends at the Déesse Fountain.

Play chess at the Vieille Bourse in the late afternoon (➤ 20).

Have a Turkish bath on Sunday—family day at the Maison Folie Wazemmes ☎ 03 20 14 34 34.

Jog around the Citadelle ramparts on Sunday morning.

Take tea and cakes at Patisserie Méert (➤ 49).

5

Other Markets

If you are not in town for the Braderie or Wazemmes, some other addresses for serious shoppers:

Marché Sébastopol
✉ place Sébastopol.
Wednesday and Saturday mornings for farm-fresh foods and a few clothes and jewellery stalls in the shadow of the theatre.

Marché du Concert
✉ place du Concert.
Sunday, Wednesday and Friday mornings this is the Vieux Lille rendezvous for serious foodies, with producers from all over the region displaying their finest from dawn.

Pétit Marché de l'Art
✉ rue Léon Trulin.
Artists and art lovers gather by the opera house on the 1st and 3rd Saturday of each month.

La Vieille Bourse
✉ place du Général de Gaulle
Second-hand book market from Tuesday to Sunday 1–7pm in 17th-century merchant exchange (➤ 20).

Marché de Noël
✉ place Rihour
Chalets selling advent wreaths, tree baubles and nativity figurines throughout December.

5

Treats for Children

All the fun of the funfair in the Bois de Boulogne in school holidays and on the place Rihour carousel all year round.

Animal magic. The Jardin Zoologique has no admission charge (➤ 12).

Roam amongst the bones of the Natural History Museum (➤ 34).

Journey into outer space at the Forum de Sciences Planetarium in Villeneuve d'Ascq (➤ 41).

Puppet shows at the Jardin Vauban and in Marionette Theatres around the metropolis.

Weekly listings from the Tourist Office.

Left: *Treasure for everyone at the Braderie*

The five point Citadelle in the Bois de Boulogne

10

Activities

The Party of the Year. Stay up all night to rummage and nosh as the streets never sleep for the 48-hour Braderie (► 10).

Lille by Night. On Wednesday nights in July and August meet at the foot of the Déesse fountain at 9pm for an after-dinner walking tour of Vieux Lille after dark. The evening ends with a beer tasting.

Cycle through the Bois. The hardy follow the cobbled paths, the wise ride under the trees. Bike hire from Localille at rue Pierre Legrand ☎ 06 88 65 10 55.

Keep a romantic rendezvous at the top floor of the tropical green-house in the Jardin des Plantes, before walking hand-in-hand by the water-falls of the monumental rose garden.

Keep your eye on the ball at Métro Bowling on the boulevard Victor Hugo ☎ 03 20 52 70 80 (► 56) or the huge Planet Bowling in Lomme ☎ 03 20 08 10 50

Swim with the tide at Villeneuve d'Ascq's tropical pool Centre Nautique Babylone ☎ 03 20 89 56 20.

Sneak in a brisk round of golf at the 9-hole Golf Lille Metropole ☎ 03 20 47 42 42. First-timers can swing with gusto on Sundays from 3–5pm.

Take a boat along the Deûle and follow the distillers' route de Genièvre to Wambrechies ☎ 03 21 39 15 15.

Bird's eye view No 1: a 15-minute helicopter flight over the city is the VIP's overview. Details from the tourist office.

Bird's eye view No 2: from December to January, a huge ferris wheel lifts passengers from the grotto in the Grand' Place to the skies. Open until 1am.

5

Places to Lunch

Expensive restaurants (► 48–50) often have lunch menus at half their evening prices.

Flam's (€)
✉ 8 rue de Pas ☎ 03 20 54 18 38. Just behind Grand' Place, the ridiculously inexpensive *flammekueche* specialist (► 49).

Le Coq Hardi (€)
✉ 44 place du Général de Gaulle ☎ 03 20 55 21 08. Tables on the Grand' Place for good simple food.

La Houblonnière (€)
✉ 42 place du Général de Gaulle ☎ 03 20 74 54 34. Family-run with regional dishes on the main square.

Aux Moules (€)
✉ 34 rue de Béthune ☎ 03 20 57 12 46. Legendary *moules-frites* in the heart of the shopping district

Brasserie Flôre (€€)
✉ 11 place Rihour ☎ 03 20 57 97 07. Popular venue between the squares.

MAISON NATALE DU GÉNÉRAL DE GAULLE ✪✪
(GENERAL DE GAULLE'S BIRTHPLACE)

On 22 November 1890 Charles de Gaulle (➤ 10) was born at his grandmother's house in the Quartier Royale. The house is now a museum dedicated to the war hero and president. On display are the Citroën DS in which he was travelling during a failed assassination attempt at Petit Clamart outside Paris, his ceremonial sword and the christening robe he wore for his baptism at the Eglise St André, across the road, the very day he was born.

MUSÉE D'ART MODERNE (➤ 15, TOP TEN)

✚ 24C5
✉ 9 rue Princesse
☎ 03 28 38 12 05
🕐 Summer: Wed–Sun 11–6, winter: Wed–Sun 10–5; closed public holidays
🚃 3, 6 Magasin
♿ Few—access to ground floor exhibition only
🍴 Cheap
↔ Vieux Lille (➤ 21)

Above: *Notre Dame de la Treille*

MUSÉE DE L'HOSPICE COMTESSE (➤ 16, TOP TEN)

NOTRE DAME DE LA TREILLE ✪✪✪

On the *îlot comtesse* site of the Counts of Flanders' château, the foundation stone of the cathedral was laid in 1854. Work was finally completed in November 1999. Though the chapel and apse were built by the end of the 19th century and the city welcomed its first bishop in 1913, building continued slowly until the project was abandoned in 1947. For decades Lille had the distinction of being a city with three-quarters of a neo-Gothic cathedral, until the architect P. L. Carlier designed a 21st-century façade. Notre Dame now has a striking frontage and piazza. The new rose window was created by Kijno, and the magnificent doors by sculptor and Holocaust survivor George Jeanclos.

✚ 25D4
✉ place Gilleson
☎ 03 20 55 28 72
🕐 Mon, Tue, Wed, Fri and Sat 10–12 and 2–6, Thu 10–6, Sun 10–1 and 3–6 (Jun–Sep open until 7)
🚃 3, 6, 9 Lion d'Or
♿ Few
🍴 Free
↔ Musée de l'Hospice Comtesse (➤ 16), Vieux Lille (➤ 21), Walk (➤ 38)

PALAIS DES BEAUX-ARTS (➤ 17, TOP TEN)

PALAIS RIHOUR ✪✪

All that remains of the 15th-century Gothic palace of the Dukes of Burgundy are a stairwell, some mullioned windows and two chapels. In the 17th century the building became the town hall, but after a fire in 1916, the remains proved too small for civic government. Today the lower chapel houses the tourist office, and the Philippe Le Bon's upper chapel with its trefoil windows, Burgundian coats of arms and vaulted ceiling, may be seen by appointment. Occasional concerts are held here. The eastern outer wall of the building is an imposing war memorial. A sense of occasion in the place Rihour is justified by at least two streets feeding the square: rue de la Vieille Comédie is named after Voltaire's visit to Lille in 1741 to premiere his play *Mohamet*, and Mozart himself performed on the site of the Hotel Bellevue.

LES PLACES (▶ 18–19, TOP TEN)

> ### DID YOU KNOW?
>
> Lille's oldest railway station, the Gare Lille-Flandres, was in fact Paris's original Gare du Nord rebuilt stone by stone. The first train from Paris to Lille carried government ministers, and two royal princes. It was blessed on arrival by the Bishop of Douai and met by the composer Hector Berlioz conducting his *Railway Cantata*, especially written for the event.

P'TIT QUINQUIN ✪

Lille has its own civic lullaby, and that lullaby even has its own statue. The song, composed in 1853 by Alexandre Desrousseaux, tells of a poor lacemaker and her child, who simply would not stop crying. At the composer's funeral, the song was played as a march, and 10 years later the town commissioned this monument to the composer. Eugene Deplechin's statue features the mother and child surrounded by the tools of her trade. Other monuments in the garden include the bust of Maréchal Foch and the flirtatious Suzanne at her bath.

Bearing the scars of a thousand hugs, the much loved statue has been clambered over by generations of schoolchildren touched by the melodramatic story of poverty and tears

---

🚩 25D3
✉ place Rihour
☎ 03 59 57 94 00
🕐 Tourist office Mon–Sat 9.30–6.30; Sun, public holidays 10–12, 2–5. Closed 1 Jan, 1 May and 25 Dec
🍴 Many cafés and restaurants outside (€–€€)
🚇 Rihour
♿ None, but ground floor access planned
🎫 Free
🔄 Les Places (▶ 18), Vieille Bourse (▶ 20), St-Maurice (▶ 37)
❓ Carousel and exhibitions in place Rihour. Starting point for guided tour bus (▶ 7) on the hour, every hour during the day.

🚩 24C3
✉ Square Foch, rue National
🚇 12 Foch

19th-Century Lille

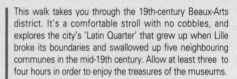

Distance
3.8km (2.4 miles)

Time
3–4 hours

Start Point
place de Général de Gaulle
✚ 24D3
🚇 Rihour

End Point
Jardin Vauban
✚ 24B3
🚌 14 Jardin Vauban

Lunch
Le Sébastopol (€€)
✉ 1 place Sébastopol
☎ 03 20 57 05 05

**Musée de l'Histoire
Naturelle et de Géologie**
✚ 25E1
✉ 19 rue de Bruxelles
☎ 03 28 55 30 80
🕐 Mon, Wed–Fri 9–12, 2–5,
Sun 10–5. Closed public
holidays
♿ Good, ground floor only
💶 Inexpensive

*Impressive skeleton in
the Musée de l'Histoire
Naturelle*

This walk takes you through the 19th-century Beaux-Arts district. It's a comfortable stroll with no cobbles, and explores the city's 'Latin Quarter' that grew up when Lille broke its boundaries and swallowed up five neighbouring communes in the mid-19th century. Allow at least three to four hours in order to enjoy the treasures of the museums.

From the Grand' Place, walk along the rue Nationale shopping street to the statue of the P'tit Quinquin (➤ 33). Turn left into the boulevard de la Liberté.

Originally named for the Empress, this thoroughfare was built in 1865 after the demolition of the city walls in 1858. Today's unassuming buildings were once the sumptuous town houses of the great industrialists and founding fathers of modern Lille, with sweeping staircases, smoking rooms and even private theatres. During the golden age of patronage and one-upmanship families could hire entire dramatic productions for their after-dinner delight. The place République was built at the same time to rival any capital city. The modern amphitheatre in the middle is actually part of the splendidly showy métro station. This is a good place to munch sandwiches and listen to buskers. The Palais des Beaux-Arts (➤ 17) is not to be missed. Across the square the grandeur of the Préfecture was inspired by the clock tower pavillion of the Louvre in Paris. One wing sports the eagle emblem of the Second Empire, the other bears an imperial N for Napoleon III.

Behind the Palais des Beaux-Arts turn right along rue Jeanne d'Arc then turn left into rue Angelier.

This area, originally home to the former Faculté des Lettres, was known as a place of study, worship and tolerance. Note the Protestant Temple, the majestic star of David window of the synagogue, and the classically inspired university buildings.

Turn right into rue de Bruxelles for the Musée de l'Histoire Naturelle et de Géologie.

A classic example of 19th-century scholarship with evocative iron walkways and spiral staircases, whale skeletons suspended from the ceilings, worthy geological exhibits and showcases featuring tableaux of stuffed wild animals in naturalistic poses.

The extravagant Théâtre Sébastapol is home to boulevard comedy and family entertainment

Rue Gosselet leads to the place Jeanne d'Arc with a statue of the heroine on horseback. Follow rue Solférino to place Le Bon.

Relish the melodramatic statue of Louis Pasteur being worshipped by the mothers of Lille. The square is dominated by the Romanesque-Byzantine church of St. Michel, surrounded by terraces of identical houses, all with private gardens and the original 100-year-old trees. Take a quick diversion into the rue Fleurus to see the Maison Coilliot (➤ 29).

Follow rue Solférino to the place Sébastopol.

The fabulous Théâtre Sébastopol is an exuberant and explosive mix of pastiche renaissance, classical and Moorish styles. It took almost 100 days to build and has given almost 100 years of pleasure to the public with a crowd-pleasing programme of operetta, popular concerts and farces. On Wednesday and Saturday mornings the car park becomes a market place (➤ 30).

Continue along rue Solférino.

At the junction with rue Nationale stands the Sacré Coeur, a confection of a church erected in gratitude for the city being spared from Prussian invasion in 1870. The stained-glass windows were created by the artists of Chartres. The spire dates from 1926 and is made of ferro-concrete. The dramatic Palais Rameau graces the end of the Solférino. Despite first impressions, the Palais is not a church, but a palatial horticultural hall, bequeathed in 1879 to the city by Auguste Rameau to host flower shows and, more recently, circuses.

Turn right and walk along the boulevard Vauban.

PORTE DE GAND ✪

Like the Porte de Roubaix (below), this looming gateway at the top of the restaurant-lined rue de Gand was built as part of the Spanish fortification of the city in 1621. From outside the city walls, the façade is grim and businesslike, on the city side of the gate, multihued brick patterns may be seen above the archways, and stone-framed windows look down the street. Vauban strengthened the defensive walls later in the century and the gardens outside the gate are home to his second line of battlements. The gateway houses the restaurant La Terrasse de Ramparts with tables on the ramparts.

PORTE DE PARIS ✪

The most striking of the three remaining gates of the city stands opposite the Hotel de Ville. Spared when the fortifications were destroyed in 1858, and again when the working class St-Sauveur quarter was razed and rebuilt in the 20th century, it takes the form of an Arc de Triomphe for Louis XIV, who had brought the city into France. It was erected 1685–92 with niches featuring the figures of Mars and Hercules symbolising War and Power, and an idealized Sun King surrounded by cherubim. Architect Simon Volant worked with Vauban on the Citadelle barracks (▶ 13). A drawbridge crosses the landscaped moat garden. Take care when you visit it as it stands on a busy roundabout.

The Porte de Paris is at the centre of a busy traffic roundabout. Take your life in your hands to reach it for a closer look!

PORTE DE ROUBAIX

The drawbridge channel and crenellations are reminders that this was the door that was slammed in the face of the Austrian Duke of Saxe-Teschen during the siege of 1792. From the rather sleazy rue de Roubaix, this long neglected gateway was deservedly rediscovered and restored during the City of Culture celebrations. Pass underneath to the Parc Matisse and see the frontage proudly displayed amongst other remnants of the walls. The two side arches were carved out in the 19th century for a tramway.

Between the hustle of the stations and the bustle of the shopping streets of the rue de Paris, the Eglise St-Maurice is a timeless sanctuary

ST-MAURICE ⭐⭐

With five high naves, this Hallekirque (or market church) has a style well adapted to the marshy Flanders soil. Dating from the 15th century and added to until the mid-19th, the church has housed works by Lille artists for 300 years. In the left transept stands a monument to the Duc de Berry, visitors should also note the organ loft and the umbrella vaulting at the centre of the church. Stained-glass windows by followers of Ingres illuminate the *Passion of Christ* and the *Martyrdom of St Maurice*. A memorial on a pillar recalls the sacrifice of British Commonwealth soldiers who fought for France's freedom. There are excellent organ recitals on summer Sundays at 4.30pm.

VIEILLE BOURSE (▶ 20, TOP TEN)

VIEUX LILLE (▶ 21, TOP TEN)

WAZEMMES (▶ 22, TOP TEN)

➕ 25E3
✉ rue de Paris
☎ 03 20 06 07 21
🕐 Mon 1.15–6, Tue–Sat 10.15–12.15 and 1.15–6, Sun 3.30–8. Guided visits Sun 3–5
🚉 Gare Lille-Flandres
♿ Few, steps to doorway
💷 Free
↔ Les Places (▶ 18–19)
❓ Regular concerts. Details from tourist office

DID YOU KNOW?

Lille's least known export is railway stations! Over 400 metal frameworks (including the Gare d'Orsay in Paris) and 2,000 railway bridges have been built at the Compagnie Mécanique Fives-Lille since 1861. The factory also constructed Cairo's bridges across the Nile.

Vieux Lille— the Old Town

Distance
2km (1.25 miles)

Time
2–3 hours

Start
Palais Rihour, place Rihour
🟦 25D3
🔲 Rihour

End
place du Général de Gaulle
🟦 25D3
🔲 Rihour

Lunch
Le Lion Bossu (€€)
✉ 1 rue St Jacques
☎ 03 20 06 06 88
🕐 Closed Sun evenings

Below: *The place Lion d'Or crossroads of the old town*

A stroll around the 17th- and 18th-century quarter. Allow two to three hours to enjoy the distractions of shop windows and quaint alleyways.

From Palais Rihour (▶ 33) cross Grand' Place (▶ 18–19). Take rue de la Bourse (where houses from 1667 are decorated with faces of chubby children and grotesque adults) to rue de la Grande Chaussée.

An iron arm above the corner shop points you in the right direction. Always the most prosperous address in town, this was the first street to be paved, linking the port to the square, then a market place. D'Artagnan (▶ 10 and 13) lived at numbers 20 and 26. At the top of the road is 3 rue des Chats Bossus—the fabulous Breton art deco mosaic frontage of l'Huîtrière, the famous fish restaurant.

Follow rue des Chats Bossus to place Lion d'Or, then bear right into place Louise de Bettignies (▶ 21). Turn back to rue de la Monnaie.

Here visit the Musée de l'Hospice Comtesse (▶ 16). Note the original shop signs of early merchants: The apothecaries' symbols at number 3, others displaying wheat, palms and dolphins. The road leads to the place du Concert market. A statue to Mayor André recalls Lille's stand against Austria in 1792 .

Take rue au Peterinck, past 18th-century weavers' houses, to the place aux Oignons.

Nothing to do with the onions sold in the nearby market, the name is a corruption of donjon (dungeon or keep). The *îlot comtesse* site of the original fortress is now home to Notre Dame de la Treille (▶ 32). Wooden bridges cross the dried canal moats.

From place Gilleson and rue du Cirque turn right into rue Basse (where there are antique dealers). Turn left into rue Esquermoise.

At number 27 end the walk with a little pampering at Meert's *salon du thé*, just a few steps from place de Gaulle.

Tourcoing

Like Roubaix (▶ 40), the town joined the Métropole Lilloise in the 1960s. Linked to Lille by the twin tramways and an extended métro service, Tourcoing is a major cultural annexe not to be missed, half an hour's ride away. The Atelier Lyrique (▶ 57) stages challenging opera productions and the November Jazz Festival holds events in public buildings and open spaces.

What to See in Tourcoing

LE FRESNOY—STUDIO NATIONAL DES ARTS CONTEMPORAINS ✪✪

Welcome to the 'In between', a remarkable space above the rooftops of a unique postgraduate arts college. The college and studio have an excellent schedule of art exhibitions and cultural events, but it was architect Bernard Tschumi's concept of the 'Great Roof' that transformed what had been the town's fun palace since 1905. A fabulous modern building hangs above the rooftops of the former fleapit cinema, dance hall, boxing ring and bowling alley. Under the new roof and above the old, metal pathways, gantries, nooks and crannies are suspended Mary Poppins style around the chimneys. Here, at sunset, locals and students stroll and canoodle on the tiles. Art films and Hollywood classics are regularly screened in two intimate cinemas and sometimes outside in the open air.

MUSÉE DES BEAUX-ARTS DE TOURCOING ✪✪✪

Follow the weekend confetti trail from the tram station to the town hall, then find this delightful museum across the square. Beyond the charming town house salons, spacious 1930s galleries display a mix of the modern and the classic: Cubists share a wall with the Brueghel school. Newspaper clippings and pamphlets on individual works are dotted around the rooms. The permanent collection is reappraised every 18 months, but you are likely to find such gems as Jean Fautrier's striking 1922 *Portrait de Ma Concierge*, and the hilariously proper *Mlle Croisette en Costume d'Amazon* by Lille artist Duran. There's usually the odd Rembrandt or Picasso, too. Almost next door is the Collectors House, at 3 square Winston Churchill, a delicious hotchpotch of every style of Flemish architecture in one building.

Tourist Office
- ✉ 9 rue de Tournai
- ☎ 03 20 26 89 03
- 🕐 Mon–Sat 9.30–12.30; 1.30–6.30. Closed Sun

- ✉ 22 rue du Fresnoy, Tourcoing
- ☎ 03 20 28 38 00
- 🕐 Mon–Fri 9–12.30 and 2–5.30
- 🍴 Bar-café (€)
- 🚇 Alsace
- ♿ Good inside the building
- 💶 Moderate
- ↔ Roubaix (▶ 40)
- ❓ Jazz and film festivals regularly use the interior and exterior spaces of Le Fresnoy

- ✉ place de l'Hotel de Ville, Tourcoing
- ☎ 03 20 28 91 60, museebeauxarts@ville-tourcoing.fr
- 🕐 Wed–Mon 1.30–6. Closed public holidays
- 🍴 In town centre near by (€–€€€)
- 🚇 Tourcoing Centre
- 🚋 Tramway Lille-Tourcoing
- ♿ Good
- 💶 Free
- ❓ Frequent jazz and classical recitals, and ballet and theatre performances

Expect the unexpected at the Musée des Beaux-Arts in Tourcoing

Right: *The art deco sunset window of the new Musée d'Art et d'Industrie reflects the building's past life as the municipal baths*

Tourist Office
☒ www.roubaixtourisme.com
☒ 12 place de la Liberté
☎ 03 20 65 31 90
🕐 Mon–Sat 9.30–6

Roubaix

Once home to the textile mills and factories of the north, Roubaix is now a lively place less than 30 minutes from Lille by tram or métro. Performances from the Ballet du Nord, major shows and concerts at the grand Colisée, and smaller theatres put on a varied schedule (➤ 56–57). Art, industry and commerce offer many attractions. Award-winning parks and gardens line the tram route into town.

What to See in Roubaix

CONDITION PUBLIQUE—MAISON FOLIE ✪✪

☒ place Faidherbe
☎ 03 28 33 57 57
🕐 Hours vary
🚌 29 to Roubaix Faidherbe
♿ Fair, but cobbles
🎭 Varies

As part of Lille 2004's cultural celebrations, a dozen abandoned buildings around Lille and the neighbouring towns were reinvented as Maisons Folies, community and arts venues. This remarkable industrial complex in Roubaix was where wool for the textile trade was once treated and packed. Now, with its internal cobbled street and cavernous galleries, it houses exhibition halls, arts space and a heritage building, with its own traditional northern *estaminet* café. The roof garden is not a new idea. In its heyday, the sloping glass roof was laid to lawn to cool the wool inside the hall. Even then, workers used to climb atop the building and bask in the sun during their lunch break. Check with tourist offices for details of concerts and themed parties.

MCARTHUR GLENN/L'USINE ✪✪✪

McArthur Glenn
☒ 44 Mail de Lannoy
☎ 03 28 33 36 00
🕐 Mon–Sat 10–7
Ⓔ Euroteleport
🚋 Tramway Lille–Roubaix

l'Usine
☒ 228 avenue Alfred Motte
☎ 03 20 83 16 20
🕐 Mon–Sat 10–7
🚇 Epeule Montesquieu, then 🚌 25 Les Hauts Chamos

True to its textile heritage, Roubaix remains a mecca for clothes shopping. McArthur Glenn opened in 1999 as the theme park of discount outlets with an idealized high street, above the Euroteleport transport hub. Here top brands sell at 30–40 per cent below usual prices. Red-coated stewards are on hand for advice and information. Most international sportswear stores are here, many French high street names and even Donaldson—the haute couture end of the Disney empire, selling green hacking tweeds with discreet Mickey Mice under the buttons. Older, less glossy, but offering rock bottom prices since 1983, is the former velvet factory known as l'Usine, an excellent factory outlet warehouse a short bus ride away.

MUSEE D'ART ET D'INDUSTRIE

Recently moved to its fabulous new home, a converted art deco swimming pool with a stunning multihued sunset window, this superb collection was established in 1835 by the great industrialists of this famous weaving town. Thousands of sample books preserve 100 years of Roubaix's creations with many more specimens of fabrics and ethnic clothing from ancient Egypt to the present day. The fine arts department, inaugurated in 1862, includes works by Ingres (the only major French artist not represented at the Palais des Beaux-Arts (► 17), Picasso and Camille Claudel. Architect Jean-Paul Philippon's celebration of the building's original life is as much a work of art as the collection's treasures. The new site features a catwalk and auditorium for fashion shows.

✉ 23 rue de l'Esperance, Roubaix
☎ 03 20 69 23 60
🕐 Tue–Thu 11–6, Fri 11–8, Sat and Sun 1–6. Closed Mon and hols
🍴 Cafés and restaurants (€€)
🚇 Euroteleport
🚋 Tramway Lille–Roubaix
♿ Good
✋ Moderate
↔ Le Fresnoy, Tourcoing (► 39)

Villeneuve d'Ascq

A new town within the metropolis, most famous for its tours of flour and linseed oil mills, and an archaeological park with reconstructed homes from the neolithic to medieval eras. Less than 10 minutes from central Lille by métro.

Mills Tour
☎ 03 20 05 49 34

Archaeological Park
☎ 03 20 47 21 99

What to See in Villneuve d'Ascq

MUSÉE D'ART MODERNE (► 15, TOP TEN)

FORUM DES SCIENCES—CENTRE FRANÇOIS MITTERAND (SCIENCE MUSEUM AND PLANETARIUM)

Science without tears in this user and family friendly exhibition centre. Themes change twice yearly, but are always fun and disarmingly speculative. What If... exhibitions on over-population, stress, future foods and other popular topics bring scientific concepts into the realm of everyday life. One department is designed for the under sixes, with storytelling and splashy, messy, hands-on activities at the weekend. The superb Planetarium has ten programmes ranging from the concept of time to life on Mars, with a preview of the evening's night sky over Lille. There is live commentary and a question and answer session with informed and helpful staff.

✉ 1 place de l'Hôtel de Ville, Villeneuve d'Ascq
☎ 03 20 19 36 36
🕐 Tue–Fri 10–5.30; Sat, Sun 2.30–6.30. Closed Mon
🍴 Café-restaurant on site (€€)
🚇 Villeneuve d'Ascq Hôtel de Ville
♿ Very good
✋ Inexpensive/moderate

The heavens on earth at the Planetarium

Tramway Touristique

☎ 03 28 38 84 21

🚌 Bus 9 from Lille to Marquette. Service runs every 15 minutes Sundays and public holidays Apr–Sep 2.30–7pm

♿ Inexpensive

Wambrechies

The *genièvre* gin town is being replanned since the distillery became a European classified heritage site. A pleasure port is under construction and roads are being moved, but life goes on. It's only a bus ride from Lille, though a vintage tramway still runs a veteran tram from the nearby town of Marquette, and a Sunday barge travels along the River Deûle from Lille to the distillery.

What to See in Wambrechies

DISTILLERIE CLAEYSSENS ✪✪

The most striking aspect of this listed distillery is the fact that it still uses the original wooden machinery constructed nearly 200 years ago. Visitors are escorted around this fascinating timewarp that produces the legendary juniper gin and an associated 40 per cent alcohol Vieux Malt that would be at home in the Highlands of Scotland. The ingenious contraptions that sift the grains, mill the flour, heat, cool and distil the spirit are all powered from one tiny engine. The story of how grain came along the canals from Belgium during Napoleon's ban on using French crops for drink, is only part of an entertaining hour's anecdotal tour of the quaint old buildings. It's followed by a bracing tasting session and a chance to buy from the distillery shop.

📧 1 rue de la Distillerie, Wambrechies

☎ 03 20 14 91 91

🕐 Guided tours daily (except public holidays) 9.30–12.30 and 1.30–5.30. Reservations essential

🍴 Cafés and restaurants in the port and town

🚌 9 Wambrechies Château

♿ Moderate

❓ Combined boat trip and distillery tour ticket available

MUSEE DE LA POUPÉE ET DU JOUET ANCIEN ✪✪
(MUSEUM OF DOLLS AND ANTIQUE TOYS)

Juliette, the last countess of Robersart, bequeathed her family château to the town, and a century later guaranteed that Wambrechies would never lose its childhood. In two child-sized galleries live Victorian dolls and their furniture, pre-cuddled playmates and even a tableau of a cathedral wedding attended by dozens of Barbies from every decade. There are train sets, castles, models, boats and comics as well as regular special exhibitions such as a century of miniature dresses made by junior readers of French fashion magazines. The museum is run by an association of private collectors, whose passion for nostalgia and belief in fairytales is bewitchingly infectious.

📧 Chateau de Robersart, Wambrechies

☎ 03 20 39 69 28

🕐 Wed, Sun and public holidays 2–6. Closed 25 Dec and 1 Jan

🍴 Cafés and restuarants in the port and town

🚌 9 Wambrechies Château

♿ Inexpensive

❓ Annual toy and dolls fair in the town each autumn

Playmates of yesteryear fêted at Wambrechies toy museum

Excursions from Lille

Lille may once have been the capital of Flanders, but today it is the capital of the Nord-Pas de Calais region, a vast area of northern France that sprawls from Belgium to Picardy.

The glorious coastline of the Côte d'Opale stretches from Dunkerque to the bay of the Somme, taking in the cliffs of the English Channel, fashionable resorts such as le Touquet, and familiar ports like Calais and Boulogne. A region rich in European history, from the Battle of Agincourt to Napoleon's Empire, with historic sites such as the Field of the Cloth of Gold and the Montreuil-sur-Mer of Victor Hugo's *Les Misérables*, there is plenty to lure the visitor away from the city centre. And don't forget, Brussels is only 40 minutes by train, and Paris just an hour away.

> *'Lille owes its new fame to the charm of its rediscovered heritage and to the warm nature it has been able to protect'*
>
> PIERRE MAUROY
> Senator and Mayor of Lille since 1973
> Former Prime Minister

Arras & Vimy Ridge

Distance
115km (71.5 miles)

Time
4 hours

Start/End Point
Lille

From Lille take the A1 motorway (towards Paris) for 19km/12 miles. At Carvin (Junction 18) join the N17 (towards Lens and Arras) for 26km/16 miles. Passing Vimy look for signs to Mémorial Canadien. Turn right into the Parc Comémoratif and drive 3km/2 miles to Memorial.

Vimy Ridge was captured by Canadian soldiers in April 1917. In the forest of the park, donated by France to Canada, each tree represents a life lost. The white cenotaph is inscribed: 'To the valour of their countrymen in the Great War and in memory of their 60,000 dead, this monument is raised by the people of Canada'.

The giant cenotaph at Vimy took 11 years to build and dominates the Douai Plain

Drive around the monument, then follow signs to trenches and tunnels (2km/1.25 miles).

Sheep graze on land pockmarked with craters that may have unexploded mines. One area has been cleared, with marked paths through the trenches of German and Allied front lines. In summer visitors may walk through tunnels behind the lines.

Lunch
La Faisanderie, Arras
✉ 45 Grand' Place
☎ 03 21 48 20 76
🕐 Tue 7–9, Wed–Sat 12–2 and 7–9. Closed Sun pm, all day Mon, Tue lunch

Turn left from car park on D55.

Pause at Neuville St. Vaast war memorial, with its plaques to resistance heroes.

Mémorial Canadien de Vimy
Tunnel tours
☎ 03 21 50 68 68
🕐 Apr–Nov 10–5.30
Free
Trenches and memorial open year round dawn–dusk

Turn right on the D49 to the crossroads at la Targette. Turn left on the D937 to the N17 (Arras). Follow the signs (Centre Ville, Places, Gare) to arrive at Grand' Place.

The glorious 17th- and 18th-century architecture here and in place des Heros was completely rebuilt according to the original plans following its wartime destruction. Under the Hôtel de Ville belfry visit the basement galleries of the old town, and the underground passages leading to World War I trenches, which once had an army railway.

Arras Underground Passages
☎ 03 21 51 26 95
🕐 May–Sep, Mon–Sat 9–6.30, Sun, hols 10–1, 2.30–6.30; Oct–Apr Mon–Sat 9–12, 1–6, Sun Hols 10–12.30, 3–6.30
Moderate

Leave Arras on the N17 for 750m/817yds, then take the N50 for 10km/6 miles to the A1 (towards Lille).

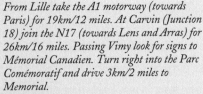

CENTRE HISTORIQUE MINIER (HISTORIC MINING CENTRE) ⚫⚫

Former miners lead visitors to the biggest mining museum in France, on tours of the site of the old Delloye pit. The striking Salle des Pendues, a combined bathhouse and locker-room, displays how clean clothes were hoisted high above the showers to keep them free of coal dust and soap. A mini-train and simulated lift ride into the tunnels provides a vivid impression of what it was like working at the coalface. Other exhibits present the daily live of miners, their wives, families and pit-ponies, and tales of tragedies and heroics. The museum also houses a fossil collection.

- ✉ Lewarde
- ☎ 03 20 95 82 82
- 🕐 Mar–Oct daily 9–5.30; Nov–Feb Mon–Sat 1–5, Sun 10–5. Closed public holidays and Jan
- 🍴 Restaurants on site (€€)
- ℹ Douai 03 27 88 26 79
- 🚉 Douai (8km/5 miles)
- 💷 Expensive, moderate in winter

DOMAINE MANDARINE NAPOLEON ⚫

A distillery and a museum dedicated to Napoleon—both transplanted to a farm just off the A1 autoroute from Lille. An arboretum and butterfly garden in the grounds hardly hint at the eccentric combination of leisure options at the new French home of the Belgian liqueur Mandarine Napoléon. One wing of the farm compound houses an eclectic private collection of Napoleonic memorabilia, including the emperor's letters, uniforms, medals and death mask. Opposite is the modern distillery offering tours and tastings. A unique feature is the lavishly furnished mansion, where guests may stay overnight enjoying the all benefits of a well-stocked kitchen and honesty bar.

- ✉ 204 rue de Burgault, Seclin
- ☎ 03 20 32 54 93
- 🕐 Tue–Sat 10–5
- 🍴 Cafés and restaurants nearby (€–€€€)
- 🚌 62, 65
- 💷 Moderate
- ❓ Accommodation available, expensive

Above: *From Austerlitz to Waterloo to the drawing room— Napoleonic memorabilia at the Napoleon museum*

St Omer

Distance
150km (93 miles)

Time
4–8 hours depending on time spent in museums

Start/End Point
Lille

Arc International
✉ Zone Industrielle RN43, Arques
☎ 03 21 12 74 74
🕐 Mon–Sat 9–10.30 and 1.30–5.30
💶 Inexpensive
❓ Visit lasts 90 minutes

Notre Dame cathedral in St Omer

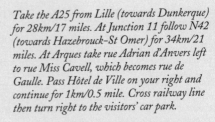

Take the A25 from Lille (towards Dunkerque) for 28km/17 miles. At Junction 11 follow N42 (towards Hazebrouck–St Omer) for 34km/21 miles. At Arques take rue Adrian d'Anvers left to rue Miss Cavell, which becomes rue de Gaulle. Pass Hôtel de Ville on your right and continue for 1km/0.5 mile. Cross railway line then turn right to the visitors' car park.

The world-famous Arc International glass and crystal factory produces 5.5 million items every day. At the Visitors Centre join the tour from furnace to factory floor.

Drive back through the town to rejoin N42 to St Omer, 3km/2 miles. Follow signs for Centre Ville. Try to park on the place Maréchal Foch in front of the Hôtel de Ville.

Take rue Dupuis to Cathédrale Notre Dame dating from 1200. Treasures include Astronomical Clock (1588) in north transept. Rues Tibuneaux and Carnot lead to Hôtel Sandelin, the 18th-century home of Viscountess of Fruges, now a museum.

From place Foch, pass a cinema on your left and follow 'Toutes Directions' to main roundabout. Take the first right (D298 towards Abbeville) to Wizernes. From double roundabout, turn back to railway crossing, right on D210 to La Coupole, 1km/0.5 miles on right.

La Coupole
☎ 03 21 12 27 27
🕐 Mon–Sat 9–6, Sun 10–7. Closed 1 week Christmas, 1 week New Year
💶 Moderate
🍴 Restaurant on site (€)
❓ Allow at least 2–3 hours

From the War to the Moon, La Coupole is a unique multimedia presentation of history's darker side. Two major exhibitions are housed in a Nazi V2 bunker. 'The Conquest of Space' follows rocket science from Hitler's planned attack on Britain to the Apollo moon landings. 'Northern France in German hands' is an emotional journey through daily life in occupied France.

Lunch
La Brasserie Audomaroise (€)
✉ 6 rue Louis Martel
☎ 03 21 88 08 80

Leaving La Coupole, turn right and right again to D198. Turn left, D210, left again on D77 for 3.5km/2 miles, turning right to the N42 for 31km/19 miles, then take the A25 towards Lille.

Where To...

Above: *Fresh eggs*
Right: *Dish of the day of the Braderie: mussels and chips*

Lille

What the locals term *bon rapport qualité-prix* is best found on the prix-fixe set price menu. Lunchtimes see even cheaper set meals, often less than half price. In Lille check out the number of Cs displayed on stickers in restaurant windows. The Business School each year reviews every restaurant in town for service, value and atmosphere. The selected establishments are graded C to CCCCC.

l'Assiette du Marché (€€€)

Old fashioned elegance in courtyard opposite the Hospice Comtesse.

⊠ 61 rue de la Monnaie ☎ 03 20 06 83 61 ⊙ Lunch, dinner. Closed Sat lunch, Mon lunch, Sun and holidays 🚇 3, 6, 9

Le Baan Thai (€€)

Top of the range Thai food served in classy surroundings.

⊠ 22 boulevard Lebas ☎ 03 20 86 06 01 ⊙ Lunch, dinner. Closed Sun dinner 🚇 13

La Baignoire (€)

Trendy modern brasserie between the Palais des Beaux Arts and the pedestrianized shopping centre of town.

⊠ 8 place Béthune ☎ 03 20 30 07 44 🚇 République

Bateau Swanny V (€€€)

Dinner cruise, with occasional karaoke on the canals between Lille and Douai.

☎ 03 27 96 39 25 ⊙ Certain evenings, phone for dates and locations

Brasserie Flore (€–€€)

Popular traditional fare.

⊠ 11 place Rihour ☎ 03 20 57 97 07 ⊙ Lunch, dinner 🚇 Rihour

La Cave Aux Fioles (€€)

Bluesy atmospheric dining room in 17th-century house. Imaginative twists on regional produce.

⊠ 39 rue de Gand ☎ 03 20 55 18 43 ⊙ Lunch, dinner. Closed Sat lunch, Sun and holidays 🚇 3, 6, 9

Chez La Vieille (€)

Typical northern country cuisine served in an intimate hop-filled dining room.

⊠ 60 rue de Gand ☎ 03 28 36 40 06 ⊙ Closed Sun, Mon 🚇 3, 6 , 9

Clémont Marot (€€€)

Gastronomy with a northern flair.

⊠ 16 rue de Pas ☎ 03 20 57 011 10 ⊙ Lunch, dinner. Closed Sun eve 🚇 Rihour

Les Compagnons de la Grappe (€)

Wine bar in a courtyard shared with neighbouring *tapas* establishment.

⊠ 26 rue Lepelletier ☎ 03 20 21 02 79 ⊙ Lunch, dinner. Closed Sun eve, Mon eve (Oct–May only) 🚇 Rihour

Le Compostelle (€€)

Lovely 16th-century building converted into a warren of quaint yet informal dining rooms, situated just off Grand' Place.

⊠ 4 rue Saint-Etienne ☎ 03 28 38 08 30 ⊙ Lunch, dinner 🚇 Rihour

Le Coq Hardi (€)

Eat and people watch from the pavement tables of this traditional bistro on the main square of Lille.

⊠ 44 pl Général de Gaulle

☎ 03 20 55 21 08 ⊙ Lunch, dinner ⊜ Rihour

La Coquille (€€)
Pretty old red brick restaurant behind the rue Nationale. Paté, duck and other farmyard fare with some good fish dishes.
✉ 60 rue Saint-Etienne ☎ 03 20 54 29 82 ⊙ Lunch, dinner. Closed Sat lunch, Sun ⊜ Rihour

La Ducasse (€)
The 1910 pianola plays old favourites, as locals sing along. Home cooking in the market quarter.
✉ 95 rue Solférino ☎ 03 20 57 34 10 ⊙ Lunch, dinner ⊜ République

L'Écume des Mers (€€)
Smart revamped seafood restaurant in quiet square behind Grand' Place.
✉ 10 rue de Pas ☎ 03 20 54 95 40 ⊙ Lunch, dinner. Closed Sun dinner, Aug ⊜ Rihour

Estaminet de la Royale (€)
Genuine Vieux Lille neighbourhood café bar for lovers of plain home cooking.
✉ 37 rue Royale ☎ 03 20 42 10 11 ⊙ Lunch. Closed Sun, holidays 🚌 3

Estaminet 'T Rijsel (€)
Warm welcome and local comfort food in this popular café/restaurant.
✉ 25 rue de Gand ☎ 03 20 15 01 59 ⊙ Lunch, dinner. Closed Sun, Mon 🚌 3, 6, 9

Les Faits Divers (€€)
Popular restaurant attracting a youthful crowd.
✉ 44 rue de Gand ☎ 03 20 21 03 63 ⊙ Lunch, dinner. Closed Sat lunch, Sun 🚌 3, 6, 9

Flam's (€)
Cheapest meal in town is the most fun. Flammekueche—that not-quite-pizza, not-quite-crêpe specialty, with sweet or savoury toppings, to eat with your fingers and wash down with a beer. Businessmen, students and families all mingle happily.
✉ 8 rue de Pas ☎ 03 20 54 18 38 ⊙ Lunch, dinner ⊜ Rihour

Les Folies de Paris (► 56)

Hippopotamus (€)
Chain grill restaurant facing the Vieille Bourse.
✉ 2 rue Faidherbe ☎ 03 28 38 95 00 ⊙ Lunch, dinner ⊜ Gare Lille-Flandres

À l'Huîtrière (€€€)
The finest restaurant in Lille turns the preparation of fish into an art form. Expensive, but worth it. The fish shop frontage is famed for its art deco tiling and mosaics.
✉ 3 rue des Chats Bossus ☎ 03 20 55 43 41 ⊙ Lunch, dinner. Closed Sun dinner 🚌 3, 6, 9

Le Jardin du Cloitre (€€)
Good quality restaurant in the cloister of the Golden Tulip Alliance Hotel.
✉ 17 quai de Wault ☎ 03 20 30 62 62 ⊙ Lunch, dinner 🚌 12

Méert (€)
Charles de Gaulle was partial to the celebrated *gaufrettes*—filled waffles—that have graced many a palace since Patisserie Méert began trading in the 1760s. The patisserie was decorated in 1839 with mirrors, balconies, caddies and caskets. The *salon du thé* behind the shop provides savoury lunchtime snacks, confectionery and a

Eat Like a Local!
Some regional dishes are found on every menu. Cheese or leek flans and *moules-frites* (mussels and chips) are staple snacks and starters. Other dishes you should look out for are: *Potjevlesch*, a cold dish of veal, rabbit and ham; *Waterzoï au poisson*, creamy sole and vegetables; *carbonade Flamande*, beer-based beef stew; *lapain aux pruneaux*, rabbit with prunes; *andouillette*, a sausage from Cambrai. Desserts include *tarte à cassonade*, brown sugar tart.

Drink Like a Local!
Beer is the tipple of choice. Bière Blonde is the equivalent to a lager. The cloudy Blanche de Lille is best served chilled with a slice of lemon. Well-known bottled brews to order include La Gueuze, Les 3 Monts and Chíti. The after-dinner spirit is *genièvre*, a whisky-like drink flavoured with juniper berries (► 42). It may be mixed with crème de cassis to make a *chuche mourette* apèritif.

49

Meet at the Meat Rack

The former wholesale market halls of Les Halles on rue Solférino is the hub of nightlife. Part student hangout, part party-animal safari park, restaurants, bars and pavements are an electrifying life force on Friday and Saturday nights. One bar, la Bucherie, a former butcher's shop, is a veritable meat-rack, other restaurants are perfect hideaways for celebrations for two. New eateries spring up with every new season, and some casualties fade away like old soldiers. But do not dismiss the area as merely the haunt of the green and trendy. There are more than a few tables well worth a detour, here and towards the Théâtre Sébastapol on the place Sébastapol itself. Around the square and along the rues Gambetta, Solférino, Puebla and their neighbours are some excellent African, Asian and Greek restaurants. Never forget that the cosmopolitan community of Lille has gastronomic cultures with roots far from Flanders.

selection of more than 80 fine specialty teas. On Sundays the people of Lille traditionally buy cakes here as gifts when visiting family.
🖂 27 rue Esquermoise ☎ 03 20 57 07 44 🕧 Elevenses, lunch and tea 🚇 Rihour

Omnia (€)

Brash brasserie serves *tartflilette* and home brewed beer in a former burlesque dance hall.
🖂 9 rue Esquermoise ☎ 03 20 57 55 66 🕧 Lunch, dinner 🚇 Rihour

Le Palais de la Bierre (€)

Smart modern café in front of the old station.
🖂 11 pl de la Gare ☎ 03 20 06 38 94 🚇 Lille-Flandres

Paul (€)

Breakfast served against the old tiles and timbers of this elegant bakery is best value in town. The upstairs dining room offers superb views.
🖂 8 rue de Paris ☎ 03 20 78 20 78 🕧 Breakfast, lunch, dinner 🚇 Rihour

Les Pecheurs d'Etaples (€€)

Appropriately opposite the old market hall, this fish restaurant specializes in preparing the day's catch from the Channel.
🖂 150 rue Solférino ☎ 03 20 40 20 38 🕧 Lunch, dinner. Closed Sunday dinner 🚇 République

La Petite Cave (€€)

Local singers deliver tributes to Piaf, Montand or faded Eurovision stars while guests tuck into wholesome northern cooking. Reservations only.
🖂 80 rue St André ☎ 03 20 06 60 66 🕧 Dinner

La Petite Cour (€)

Busy courtyard café popular with students.
🖂 17 rue Saint-Etienne ☎ 03 20 51 52 81 🕧 Lunch, dinner. Closed Sun, Mon 🚇 Rihour

La Robe des Champs (€)

Potatoes with every topping imaginable.
🖂 10 rue Faidherbe ☎ 03 20 55 13 74 🕧 Lunch, dinner 🚇 Lille Flandres

Sebastapol (€€)

Excellent cuisine served in the ivy covered house opposite the theatre.
🖂 1 place Sébastopol ☎ 03 20 57 05 05 🕧 Lunch, dinner. Closed Sat lunch, Sun (Aug), two weeks in Aug 🚇 République

Le Square (€)

Noisy, friendly, informal buzz of crowds who like good honest food in Vieux Lille.
🖂 52 rue Basse ☎ 03 20 74 16 17 🕧 Lunch, dinner. Closed Mon dinner, Sun and Aug 🚇 Rihour

La Terrasse Des Remparts (€€)

Smart dining room right in the fortified Porte de Gand itself.
🖂 Logis de la Porte de Gand ☎ 03 20 06 74 74 🕧 Lunch, dinner 🚇 3, 6, 9

Les Trois Brasseurs (€)

All beers brewed on site, and rich northern foods keep this place packed from first to last. First timers should order the *Palette de Dégustation* to sample the blanche, *ambrée*, *brune* and *blonde* beers in one sitting.
🖂 22 place de la Gare ☎ 03 20 06 46 25 🕧 Lunch, dinner 🚇 Lille-Flandres

Lille

Best Hotel (€)
Basic hotel at the gateway to Sunday morning's market of Wazemmes.
✉ 66 rue Littré ☎ 03 20 54 00 02, fax 03 20 54 00 06
Ⓜ Gambetta

Bellevue (€€)
Renovated bedrooms, with marbled en-suites, have views over Grand' Place. Piano bar.
✉ 5 rue Jean Roisin ☎ 03 20 57 45 64, fax 03 20 40 07 93 Ⓜ Rihour

Carlton (€€€)
Comfortable, slightly old fashioned Grand Hotel on a key corner site overlooking the place du Théâtre.
✉ 3 rue de Paris ☎ 03 20 13 33 13, fax 03 20 51 48 17 Ⓜ Lille-Flandres

Chagnot (€)
Basic, clean, soundproofed station hotel.
✉ 24 place de la Gare ☎ 03 20 74 11 87, fax 03 20 74 08 23 Ⓜ Lille-Flandres

Citadines Lille Centre (€€)
Well-equipped self-catering studios in Euralille, ideal for cooking the wonderful fresh food from the market.
✉ 83 avenue Willy Brandt ☎ 08 25 01 03 63 Ⓜ Lille-Flandres

Flandres-Angleterre (€)
Friendly, family-run hotel opposite the Gare Lille Flandres. Soundproof.
✉ 15 place de la Gare ☎ 03 20 06 04 12, fax 03 20 06 37 76 Ⓜ Lille-Flandres

Golden Tulip Alliance (€€€)
Contemporary business class conversion of 17th-century convent near the Bois de Boulogne.
✉ 17 quai de Wault ☎ 03 20 30 62 62, fax: 03 20 42 94 25
☎ 12

L'Hermitage Gantois (€€€)
As much an historic monument as an hotel, the restoration of this cluster of 15th-centruy hospice buildings, now the city's only 4-star luxury hotel, reveals beautiful courtyards, library and chapel. Call for information on weekly guided tours. Hotel guests and visitors to the hotel foyer bar get to pry for free.
✉ 224 rue de Paris ☎ 03 20 85 30 30; www.hotels-slih.com
Ⓜ Mairie de Lille

Holiday Inn Express (€€)
A chain hotel at the heart of the Solferino party district, and convenient for the weekend markets.
✉ 75 bis rue Gambetta ☎ 03 20 57 14 24, fax 03 20 57 14 24
Ⓜ République

Lille Europe (€€)
Clean basic rooms in the Euralille centre, next to the international station.
✉ avenue le Corbusier ☎ 03 28 36 76 76, fax 03 28 36 77 77
Ⓜ Lille-Europe

Mercure Le Royal (€€)
Chain hotel tucked away between the Opera House and old town.
✉ 2 boulevard Carnot ☎ 03 20 14 71 47 Ⓜ Lille-Flandres

De La Paix (€€)
A warm welcome to neat rooms with framed art exhibition posters, just steps from the squares.
✉ 46 bis rue de Paris ☎ 03 20 54 63 93, fax 03 20 63 98 97
Ⓜ Rihour

Prices
Prices indicated are per room:

€	under €40
€€	€40–€60
€€€	over €60

Bon Weekend en Ville
Guests staying Friday and Saturday, or Saturday and Sunday, may enjoy two nights' accommodation for the price of one at most of the city's hotels. Visitors using the Bon Weekend deal also enjoy two-for-the price-of-one offers on museum passes and the excellent one-hour minibus tour of the city. Stays must be booked eight days in advance. Details from tourist offices.

Shopping A–Z

Shopping Areas
Grand' Place is the centre of the shopping world. The pedestrian area to the south (rues Neuve and Béthune) has most high-street names cheek by jowl with cinemas in streets garlanded with hanging baskets and ornamented by some delightful art deco architecture high above the shop fronts. Towards the stations, the rue Faidherbe is home to discount shoe and book shops. Beyond lies the Euralille shopping complex (► 14) with twins of many town centre stores. West along the rue Nationale is the Printemps department store, and north of the square is Vieux Lille (► 21) for smart boutiques and galleries where elegance comes at a price. Farther afield, the Gambetta-Wazemmes quarter welcomes budget shoppers.

Chocolate Passion
Find unusual edible souvenirs from chocolate mobile phones to the giant coins amongst the more conventional sweets.
✉ 67, rue Nationale
☎ 03 20 54 74 42;
www.chocolatpassion.com
🚇 Rihour

Antiques

Antique Shop
Nineteenth-century furniture a specialty.
✉ 16 rue Basse ☎ 03 20 51 52 97

Claude Le Mevel
Specialists in antique tableware.
✉ 12 rue Basse ☎ 03 20 31 07 08

André Davioud
Eighteenth-centruy furniture and charming faïence.
✉ 8 rue de la Baignerie
☎ 03 20 30 16 97

La Marbrerie
Clocks, paintings and mirrors from Lille's 17th- to 18th-century heyday in a charming environment.
✉ 61–63 rue Léornard Danel
☎ 03 20 42 14 77

Parnethou
Candelabra and ornaments.
✉ 23 rue Lepelletier ☎ 03 20 55 70 23

Art

Atelier Un Vrai Semblance
Guillaume Moisson is one of the last of the great copyists. If you find a Renoir, Cezanne or Van Gogh that you simply must have, simply commission M. Moisson to paint a perfect copy in his studio behind Notre Dame de la Treille. A Monet for €750, a Caravaggio for €900 perhaps.
✉ 3 rue au Peterinck ☎ 03 20 15 08 99

Books

Le Furet du Nord
The biggest bookshop in continental Europe is an instiution on Grand' Place. Half a million volumes in stock. A good travel and international section, and multimedia department
✉ place Charles de Gaule
☎ 03 20 78 43 43 🚇 Rihour

FNAC
Books, hi-fi, photographic and even concert tickets for live performances form the local branch of the nation's leading leisure store. Entrance via Voix du Nord building on Grand' Place.
✉ 20 rue St Nicolas ☎ 03 20 15 58 15 🚇 Rihour

Maxi-Livres
Bargain basement priced recipe and coffee-table books. Many branches around town.
☎ 54 rue Faidherbe ☎ 03 20 78 10 87 🚇 Lille-Flandres

Chocolates

Benoît Chocolatier
Lille's master chocolate maker.
✉ 77 rue de la Monnaie ☎ 03 20 31 69 03

Au Chat Bleu
The famous chocolate shop of Le Touquet comes to the Vieille Bourse.
✉ 3 rue des Manneliers ☎ 03 20 15 01 73 🚇 Rihour

Chocolate Passion
Unusual edible souvenirs.
✉ 67, rue Nationale
☎ 03 20 54 74 42;
www.chocolatpassion.com
🚇 Rihour

Léonidas
Popular Belgian chocolates.
✉ 49 rue Faidherbe ☎ 03 20 06 06 71. 🚇 Lille-Flandres

Neuhaus
Top Belgian chocolates without crossing the border.
✉ 13 rue du Sec Arembault
☎ 03 20 54 29 29 🚇 Lille-Flandres

Department Stores

Printemps
Parisian department store behind the tourist office.
✉ 41–45 rue Nationale
☎ 03 20 63 62 00 🚇 Rihour

Fashion: Boutiques and Accessories

Adéquat
Shoes at bargain prices.
✉ 2 rue des Ponts de Comines
☎ 03 20 78 14 60 🚇 Lille-Flandres

Benjamin
Hats and gloves supplied to the beautiful since 1926.
✉ 45 rue de Béthune ☎ 03 20 54 69 67 🚇 Rihour

Constance de Gonidec
Exquisite bridal gowns made to measure by Lille designer.
✉ 1 pl Oignons ☎ 03 20 06 44 45 🕐 Mon-Fri by appointment only, Sat 3-7 🚌 3 , 6 , 9

La Griffe
Second-hand designer wear at absolutely fabulous prices.
✉ 27 rue de la Barre ☎ 03 20 57 47 20 🕐 Closed Wed
🚌 3, 6

Hermès
Those famous scarves.
✉ 8 rue de la Grande Chaussée
☎ 03 20 51 44 51 🚇 Rihour

Jour et Nuit Création
Cutting-edge evening wear.
✉ 27 rue Lepelletier ☎ 03 20 51 20 30

Lancel
Ultimate accessories.
✉ 46–50 place de Gaulle
☎ 03 20 31 00 78 🚇 Rihour

Mad Man
Budget menswear is on offer here.
✉ 6 rue Faidherbe ☎ 03 20 31 10 32

Menthe Verte
Young, loud and trendy.
✉ 57 rue de Béthune ☎ 03 20 54 02 43 🚇 Rihour

Michel Ruc
Ladies choose local designers such as Anne Demeulemeester. Upstairs for menswear.
✉ 23–5 rue des Chats Bossus
☎ 03 20 15 96 16

N&B
Nathalie Sarazin's superb range of hats.
✉ 6 rue JJ Rousseau ☎ 03 20 42 19 79

Phildar
Cool menswear.
✉ 61 rue de Béthune ☎ 03 20 74 77 61 🚇 Rihour

Rouge
On the fringes of Vieux Lille, young European designers offer underwear, shirts, jackets and shoes.
✉ 15 rue de la Clef ☎ 03 20 74 19 20

Vents du Nord
Breton pullovers and Nordic winterwear.
✉ 41 rue de la Monnaie
☎ 03 20 31 69 33

7ème Compagnie
Army surplus wear for the hardcore clubber.
✉ 11 rue Jean Sans Peur
☎ 03 20 54 39 63

Meet the Stewards
Easily recognized by their smart yellow jackets and polo shirts, the town centre stewards travel in pairs. They are armed with directories and mobile phones to answer any sightseeing or shopping enquiry. The three most frequently requested destinations: Palais des Beaux-Arts, Vieux Lille and Wazemmes market.

Discount Clothing
As Europe's busiest mail order clothing centre, the metropolis has an international reputation as the best value shopping centre in northern Europe. The two main factory outlets in Roubaix, McArthur Glenn and l'Usine (➤ 40), offer designer clothes at 30–50 per cent discount all year round. In Lille itself several outlets near Grand' Place sell bargain sportswear and casual outfits.

Les Vins Gourmands
Wines and gifts for wine buffs
✉ 33 rue Esquermoise
☎ 03 20 30 12 20 🖷 12

Fashion: Large Sizes

Capel
Grandeur for men.
✉ 88 rue Nationale ☎ 03 20 57 48 17 🚇 Rihour

Je m'Aime en Ronde
Open on Sundays for stylish designs.
✉ 318-320 rue Gambetts
☎ 03 20 54 50 82 🚇 Rihour

Etre Ronde en Couleurs
Fun and pretty outfits in this shopping mall.
✉ passage des Tanneurs, 80 rue de Paris ☎ 03 20 54 39 44 🚇 Rihour

XX Elle
Style for the statuesque.
✉ 27 rue Nationale ☎ 03 20 15 14 79 🚇 Rihour

Fashion: Children

Gap Kids
International brand name for pampered kids.
✉ 50 rue de Béthune ☎ 03 20 15 98 00 🚇 Rihour

Vert Baudet
Bright hues for babies and mums-to-be.
✉ 15 rue de Paris ☎ 03 20 06 63 49 🚇 Rihour

Food and Wine

Art des Vins
Wisdom and wine from the cellar master.
✉ 15 rue de la Collégiale ☎ 03 20 51 35 18 ⓘ Sun am

Carrefour
The hypermarket flags regional food and drink with a heart-shaped logo.
✉ Euralille ☎ 03 20 15 56 00 🚇 Lille-Europe

Comtesse du Barry
An excellent range of pâtés and foies gras is on sale here.
✉ 21 rue Esquermoise ☎ 03 20 54 00 43

Leroy Boulangerie
Bakery for great breakfast croissants.
✉ 118 rue Esquermoise ☎ 03 20 55 35 55

Paul
This bakery has branches all over town, but the prettiest one is in rue de Paris (➤ 50).
ⓘ 7am–midnight

Philippe Olivier
One of the finest cheese masters in France.
✉ 3 rue du Curé Saint Etienne ☎ 03 20 74 96 99 🚇 Rihour

Pierre Champion
Foie gras a speciality.
✉ 8 place de Gaulle ☎ 03 20 13 93 13 🚇 Rihour

Les Vins Gourmands
Wines and gifts.
✉ 33 rue Esquermoise ☎ 03 20 30 12 20 🖷 12

Gifts

Artisanat Monastique
Tasteful ecclesiastic-themed gifts from candles to textiles.
✉ Parvis Notre Dame de la Treille ☎ 03 20 55 22 19

La Carterie
Humorous gifts, from T-shirts to cartoon clocks.
✉ Euralille ☎ 03 20 13 13 73 🚇 Lille-Europe

Christofle
Upmarket tableware, by royal appointment.
✉ 48 rue Grande Chaussée ☎ 03 20 51 46 20 🚇 Rihour

Dinner Chez Soi
Tableware and wedding presents.
✉ 2 rue du Cirque ☎ 03 28 36 82 45 🚇 Rihour

Eté Country
Gifts for the garden
✉ 27 rue des Vieux Murs ☎ 03 20 78 06 53 🚊 3, 6 or 9

Homme Moderne
Gadgets and gizmos for the chaps.
✉ Galerie Grand' Place, pl du Général de Gaulle ☎ 03 20 13 96 66 🚇 Rihour

Loisir et Création
Fantastic crafts shop.
✉ Euralille ☎ 03 20 51 39 01 🚇 Lille-Europe

Nord Maquette
Boys' toys and model aeroplanes.
✉ 28 rue du Sec Arembault ☎ 03 20 14 90 80 🚇 Rihour

Nature et Découverte
Environmentally friendly pampering products.
✉ Euralille ☎ 03 20 78 01 00 🚇 Lille-Europe

Pomme Cannelle
Exquisite plants and floral gifts.
✉ 5 rue Curé St-Etienne ☎ 03 20 06 83 06 🚇 Rihour

La Puce à L'Oreille
Vintage furnishings.
✉ 10 pl Louise de Bettignies ☎ 03 28 36 28 28 🚇 Rihour

Jewellery

Cartier
Fine jewellery.
✉ 17 rue Esquermoise ☎ 03 20 54 82 82

Perreux
The oldest jewellers in Lille.
✉ 13 rue de la Bourse ☎ 03 20 55 06 49 🚇 Rihour

Lingerie

Orcanta
✉ Euralille ☎ 03 20 55 23 36 🚇 Lille-Europe

Markets (► 22 & 38)

Music

FNAC
Everything from CDs to hi-fis and much more all under one roof (► 52).

Saturn
Home entertainment systems in the shopping mall opposite the station.
✉ Euralille ☎ 03 28 36 60 00 🚇 Lille-Europe

Perfumes

Parfumerie du Soleil d'Or
Friendly attentive service.
✉ 4 rue Esquermoise ☎ 03 20 55 31 20

Séphora
Excellent range of perfumes and cosmetics.
✉ Euralille ☎ 03 20 14 99 50

Open Late

Le Royal Primeur
Late-night grocers.
✉ 17 rue Royale ☎ 03 20 55 99 86 🕐 Every day 10am–2am. Closed Sun am

Le Bistrot de la Voûte
Cigarettes and phone cards on the Grand' Place.
✉ 60 place de Gaulle ☎ 03 20 13 86 76 🕐 Mon to Fri 7am–2am, Sat 9am–2am, Sun 10am–2am

Essential addresses for bargain hunters with no need for a posh label:

Tati
Sweaters for the price of a cup of coffee, slippers for less than a beer. Childrens' wear, menswear, ladies' wear and jewellery at ridiculous prices. Wedding dresses for less than the cost of a hotel room! Tati is an institution, although you have to sift through the dross for the gems.
✉ 12–14 rue Faidherbe ☎ 03 20 74 00 00 🚇 Lille-Flandres

Ecoshop
✉ 3 rue Gambetta ☎ 03 20 54 26 99 🚇 République

24-Hour Petrol

ELF Casino
Wazemmes
✉ 365 boulevard Victor Hugo ☎ 03 20 40 03 00

Esso
Near Mairie de Lille métro station
✉ 72 avenue du Président Kennedy ☎ 03 20 52 14 67

Nightlife, Music & Theatre

Lille Happening

On any Saturday night in Lille there is a choice of over 100 performances in clubs, theatres, opera houses and cinemas. With arts and music festivals throughout the year spilling over from other towns in the conurbation, and excellent public transport services running until midnight, the weekly listings magazine *Sortir* is the essential companion for planning a night out in or around the city. It's published every Wednesday and free from tourist offices.

Check with the tourist office for listings of concerts in churches and public buildings.

Bowling

Metro Bowling
Popular venue for all ages.
✉ 17/25 boulevard Victor Hugo ☎ 03 20 52 70 80 ⏰ Every day 10am–1am

Cabaret

Aux Rêves d'Adam et Eve
Showgirls and magic.
✉ 8 rue de Courtrai ☎ 03 20 06 04 14; www.auxrevesdadam.com

Les Folies de Paris
Cage aux Folles-style floor show where the boys are Diana Ross, Piaf and Celine Dion and the girls are Michael Jackson. Dinner and glamour.
✉ 52 avenue du Peuple Belge ☎ 03 20 06 62 64 ⏰ Tue–Sat 8pm, Sun 1pm

Nightclubs

Serious clubbers cross the border into Belgium, but there are several good addresses in town. Often admission is free, but drinks cost more than double the price charged in bars.

Le Duke's Club
Over 25's hangout.
✉ 6 rue Gosselet ☎ 03 20 52 97 98 ⏰ Thu–Sat 9pm–4am

Le Java
Lively disco.
✉ 46 rue Arras ☎ 03 20 52 92 97 ⏰ 11pm–4am

L'Opéra Night
The hottest address in town.
✉ 84 rue de Trévise ☎ 03 20 88 37 25 ⏰ Tue–Thu 9pm–4am, Fri–Sat 9–5

La Scala
Disco bar of the moment.
✉ 32 place Bettignies ☎ 03 20 42 10 60 ⏰ 10pm–4am

La Tchouka
Mixed straight and gay crowd party til late.
✉ 80 rue de Barthélémy Delespaul ☎ 03 20 14 37 50 ⏰ Fri–Sat 11pm–6am

Music Venues

L'Aeronef
Youth music venue for concerts and performance.
✉ av Willy Brand ☎ 03 28 38 50 50

Biplan
Popular concert venue.
✉ 19 rue Colbert ☎ 03 20 12 91 11

Blue Note
Bar with live rock music – mixed crowd.
✉ 8 place St-André ☎ 03 20 55 28 62

Colisée
The big variety theatre for superstar concerts, touring musicals and Ballet du Nord.
✉ rue de l'Epaule, Roubaix ☎ 03 20 24 50 51

Le Grand Mix
From classic blues to more modern performancees, this venue presents the best of local talent.
✉ place Notre-Dame, Tourcoing ☎ 03 20 70 10 00

Le Splendid
Very popular venue for music, comedy, shows and dance.
✉ 1 place du Mont de Terre ☎ 30 20 56 46 16

Le Tri Postal
Former postal sorting office next to the station is now

Music & Theatre

occasional concert venue.
📧 **av Willy Brandt** ☎ 08 90 39 2004

Zénith Arena
A 7,000 seat venue for rock concerts and supershows.
📧 **1 boulevard des Cités Unies**
☎ 03 20 14 15 16

Jazz

Le 30
City centre jazz club by the Vieille Bourse.
📧 **30 rue de Paris** ☎ 03 20 30 15 54 🕐 Mon–Sat 9pm–4am

Classical Music & Dance

Atelier Lyrique de Tourcoing
Superb intimate ensemble productions of famous operas and less familiar works.
☎ 03 20 70 66 66

Ballet du Nord
Based in Roubaix with classical and contemporary repertoire.
☎ 03 20 24 66 66

Danse à Lille
Contemporary dance companies, both local and international.
📧 **6 rue Jean Roisin** ☎ 03 28 52 42 42

Opera de Lille
Beautifully restored opera house in the heart of the city.
📧 **pl du Théâtre** ☎ 03 28 38 40 40; www.opera-lille.fr 📱 12

Orchestre Nationale de Lille
World-class concerts directed by Jean-Claude Casadesus in venues around the region.
☎ 03 20 12 82 40

Theatre

Grand Bleu
Young experimental productions.
📧 **36 avenue Marx Dormoy**
☎ 03 20 09 88 44

Le Prato
Dynamic international company.
📧 **6 allée de la Filature** ☎ 03 20 52 71 24

Rose des Vents
Theatre, music and dance from many cultures.
📧 **Boulevard Van Gogh, Villeneuve d'Ascq** ☎ 03 20 61 96 90

Théâtre de la Découverte à la Verrière
A favourite with young audiences for cutting-edge new work.
📧 **28 rue Alphonse Mercier**
☎ 03 20 54 96 75

Théâtre du Nord
Stuart Seide's company is the National Theatre of northern France. Excellent productions from Shakespeare and Molière to Beckett.
📧 **place de Gaulle** ☎ 03 20 14 24 24

Théâtre Sébastopol
Boulevard comedies, concerts and operetta.
📧 **Place Sébastopol** ☎ 03 20 54 44 50

ZEM Théâtre
Community performance space of the Wazemmes quarter.
📧 **38 rue d'Anvers**
☎ 03 20 54 13 4

Ciné-Cité
Lille has a passionate love affair with the cinema. One out-of-town multiplex alone, the Kinépolis at Lomme, has 23 screens! In the town centre are scores more cinema screens, mostly along the pedestrianized rue de Béthune, with a multi-screen art house, the Majestic on rue Pont des Comines. Non-French films are shown both in dubbed and subtitled versions (v.o. are subtitled, v.f. are dubbed).
Film buffs will enjoy festivals at the Palais des Beaux-Arts cinema Le Garance ☎ 03 20 15 92 20, Le Fresnoy (▶ 39) and the Lille Short Film Festival (▶ 58).

What's On When

Check First!
Dates and venues of events listed here are liable to change, so do check with the tourist office for final details.

November–April
Festival Mozart: Concerts and operas in venues in and around the city.

February
Tourissima: The International tourism and leisure fair.

April
Foire Internationale de Lille: International fair celebrated in the streets and at the table.
Paris-Roubaix: Legendary cycle race at the begining of the month.
Journées des Villes Fortifiées: The Citadelle and 13 other fortresses open their doors to the public on the 4th weekend.

May
Montgolfiades: Hot air balloon meeting at the Champs de Mars.
Film Festival: International competition for short films.

June
Fêtes de Lille: Citywide celebrations with street events in each quarter.
Fête de la Musique: 21 June. National Music Day with free concerts.
Gay Pride: 3rd weekend. Concerts and partying in Grand' Place.

July
Bastille Day: 14 July. Dancing in the streets and fireworks in the Bois de Boulogne.

September
Half-Marathon: 1st weekend. Launches Braderie celebration.
Braderie de Lille: 1st weekend. Europe's biggest flea market. In the first weekend in September 1 million visitors descend on Lille for Europe's largest flea market and street party. The city sets out its stalls and householders sell bric-à-brac and jumble along 200km (124 miles) of pavements. The custom dates from the Middle Ages when valets sold their master's clothes once a year. Special maps are provided by the tourist office and public transport runs all night. It's traditionally an opportunity for parents of growing children to upgrade wardrobes, and for victims of burglaries over the past 12 months to scour the streets to buy back their lost treasures for a pittance. Another tradition is the single menu—mussels and chips.
European Toy Collector's Fair at Wambrechies.
Journées du Patrimoine: 3rd weekend. Historic monuments, private buildings and classic institutions open to the public.

October–November
Tourcoing Jazz Festival: Music overflows the city limits as far away as Belgium.

November
Festival de Lille: Major international arts festival pays homage to a different nation each year.
Transculturelles: Roubaix hosts festival of theatre, dance and music.

December
Christmas market and ferris wheel: on the squares of central Lille throughout Advent.

Practical Matters

Above: *All the world comes to Lille for the Braderie*
Right: *The welcoming face of Eurostar*

TIME DIFFERENCES

GMT	France	Germany	USA (NY)	Netherlands	Spain
12 noon	→ 1pm	→ 1pm	← 7am	→ 1pm	→ 1pm

PLAN YOUR TRIP

ARRIVING

There are direct Eurostar rail services from London (taking 1 hour 40 minutes) and Ashford (1 hour), high speed Thalys trains from Brussels (38 minutes) and TGV routes from Paris Charles de Gaulle Airport (1 hour) to Lille-Europe station (☎ Eurostar 020 7922 2055 in Britain). Motorists use Eurotunnel and ferry services to Calais, 112km (70 miles) to Lille on motorways A16 - A25, 222km (138 miles) from Paris on A1. Lille Lesquin airport (☎ 03 20 49 68 68) handles many international and domestic services with regular shuttle bus to Lille-Europe Station.

Lille Lesquin Airport Distance to city centre	**Journey times**
 12 kilometres **(7.5 miles)**	15 minutes 10 minutes

MONEY

The euro (€) is the official currency of France. There are banknotes for 5, 10, 20, 50, 100, 200 and 500 euros, and coins for 1, 2, 5, 10, 20 and 50 cents, and 1 and 2 euros. Euro traveller's cheques are widely accepted.

TIME

 France is one hour ahead of Greenwich Mean Time (GMT+1), but from late March, when clocks are put forward one hour, until late October, French Summer Time (GMT+2) operates.

CUSTOMS

 YES
From another EU country for personal use (guidelines):
800 cigarettes, 200 cigars, 1 kilogram of tobacco
10 litres of spirits (over 22%)
20 litres of aperitifs
90 litres of wine, of which 60 litres can be sparkling wine
110 litres of beer

From a non-EU country for your personal use, the allowances are:
200 cigarettes OR
50 cigars OR 250 grams of tobacco
1 litre of spirits (over 22%)
2 litres of intermediary products (eg sherry) and sparkling wine
2 litres of still wine
50 millilitres of perfume
250 millilitres of eau de toilette
The value limit for goods is €175.

Travellers under 17 years of age are not entitled to the tobacco and alcohol allowances.

 NO
Drugs, firearms, ammunition, offensive weapons, obscene material, unlicensed animals.

| POLICE 17 |
| FIRE 18 |
| AMBULANCE 15 |
| HOSPITAL 03 20 44 59 62 |

WHEN YOU ARE THERE

TOURIST OFFICES

- Office du Tourism
  Palais Rihour
  Place Rihour
  BP 205, 59002 Lille Cedex
  ☎ 03 59 57 94 00
  Fax 03 20 21 94 20
  ⓘ Mon–Sat 10–6, Sun,
  holidays 10–12, 2–5

- Point Info Tourisme
  Lille-Lesquin Airport
  ⓘ Mon–Fri 7am–9pm

- Point Info Tourisme
  Lille-Europe Station
  ⓘ Mon–Fri 7am–10pm;
  Sat 9.30–6.30, Sun 10–1,
  2–6

For sites and attractions in the region:

- Comité Régional du
  Tourisme
  6 place Mendés France
  59800 Lille
  ☎ 03 20 14 57 57

NATIONAL HOLIDAYS

J	F	M	A	M	J	J	A	S	O	N	D
1		(1)	(1)	3(4)	(1)	1	1			2	1

1 Jan	New Year's Day
Mar/Apr	Easter Sunday and Monday
1 May	Labour Day
8 May	VE Day
May	Ascension Day
May/Jun	Whit Sunday and Monday
14 July	Bastille Day
15 Aug	Assumption Day
1 Nov	All Saints' Day
11 Nov	Remembrance Day
25 Dec	Christmas Day

Banks, businesses, museums and most shops,
except *boulangeries* (bakeries), are closed on these
days.

OPENING HOURS

○ Shops	● Museums/Monuments
● Offices	○ Churches
● Banks	● Pharmacies

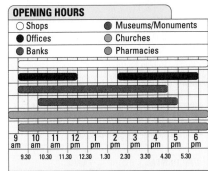

9 am	10 am	11 am	12 pm	1 pm	2 pm	3 pm	4 pm	5 pm	6 pm
	9.30	10.30	11.30	12.30	1.30	2.30	3.30	4.30	5.30

In addition to times shown above, some smaller shops
close between noon and 2pm, all day Sunday and, in
certain cases, Monday. Department stores remain
open until 7.30pm. Food shops open 7–1.30 and 4.30–8.
Shops in Euralille open 10–8 (9pm on Saturdays).
Hypermarkets 9am–10pm. Shops in the Gambetta-
Wazemmes district open Sunday mornings until noon.
Some banks in the central area open Saturday
mornings, but most close weekends. Museum opening
times vary (see individual listings), national museums
close Tuesday and regional museums usually close
Mondays.

PUBLIC TRANSPORT

 Internal Flights Services to Paris and many regional and European airports (► 60, **Arriving**)

 Trains Lille is the principal hub, outside Paris, for TGV high speed rail services around France and northern Europe. Connecting trains to southern and western France meet Eurostar services from the UK at Lille-Europe station (► 60, **Arriving**). Other regional routes and trains from the Champagne region and the East arrive at Lille-Flandres station.

 Buses The regional bus network serves all districts of Lille and its surrounding towns, up to and across the Belgian border. There are 34 routes in central Lille, and 37 suburban services. Most buses leave from the place des Buisses between the two railway stations. The tramway runs two routes from its underground terminus at Gare Lille-Flandres to Tourcoing and Roubaix.

 Métro Two métro lines from CHR-B Calmette to 4 Cantons, and St Philibert to Fort de Mons, run automatic driverless trains above and below ground, linking Lille with its principal neighbours and serving key areas within the city centre. Many central stations have glass security doors shielding the platform from the tracks.

Tickets Any single journey can be taken using one or all of the bus, tram or métro lines. Tickets are sold singly, in carnets of 10 or as a one-day *Passe Journée*. Services run from around 6AM to midnight, with a limited night bus network. No public transport operates on 1 May. Information, tickets and assistance available at Lille-Flandres Station. ☎ 08 20 42 40 40.

CAR RENTAL

All major car rental firms have offices at the airport and by the main stations. There are ten large car parks in central Lille as well as pay-and-display street parking. Carrefour hypermarket at Euralille offers free parking to shoppers spending over a stated amount.

TAXIS

More than 150 registered taxis work day and night in Lille. Ranks are at stations and key points in the town. Taxis showing two lights on their roof are available for hire. Bookings ☎ 03 20 06 06 06, 03 20 06 64 00, 03 20 55 20 56. Taxi guided tours from the tourist office.

DRIVING

 Speed limits on toll motorways (*autoroutes*) **130kph/80mph** (wet: **110kph/ 68mph**). Non-toll motorways and dual carriageways: **110kph/68mph** (wet: **100kph/ 62mph**). Paris ring road (*périphérique*): **80kph/50mph**.

 Speed limits on country roads: **90kph/56mph** (**80kph/50mph** when wet)

 Speed limits on urban roads: **50kph/31mph**

 Seat belts must be worn in front seats at all times and in rear seats where fitted.

 Random breath-testing is common. Never drive under the influence of alcohol.

 Leaded petrol is sold as *essence super* (98 octane). Unleaded is available in two grades: *essence sans plomb* (95 octane) and *essence super sans plomb* (98 octane). Diesel (*Gasoil* or *Gazole*) is also readily available. Lille has two 24-hour petrol stations (► 55).

 Carry a red warning triangle. Place this 30m (33yds) behind the car in the event of a breakdown. On motorways ring from emergency phones (every 2km/1.2 miles) to contact the local breakdown service. Off motorways, the police will advise on local breakdown services

DRIVE ON THE RIGHT

TOILETS CHARGE

★★
★★

CLOTHING SIZES

UK	Rest of Europe	USA	
36	46	36	
38	48	38	
40	50	40	Suits
42	52	42	
44	54	44	
46	56	46	
7	41	8	
7.5	42	8.5	
8.5	43	9.5	Shoes
9.5	44	10.5	
10.5	45	11.5	
11	46	12	
14.5	37	14.5	
15	38	15	
15.5	39/40	15.5	Shirts
16	41	16	
16.5	42	16.5	
17	43	17	
8	34	6	
10	36	8	
12	38	10	Dresses
14	40	12	
16	42	14	
18	44	16	
4.5	38	6	
5	39	6.5	
5.5	39	7	Shoes
6	39	7.5	
6.5	40	8	
7	41	8.5	

TELEPHONES

All telephone numbers in France comprise ten digits. There are no area codes. Most kiosks take phonecards (*télécartes*) sold in units of 50 or 120 units at post offices, tobacconists and newsagents.

International Dialling Codes

From France to:

UK:	00 44
Germany:	00 49
USA & Canada:	00 1
Netherlands:	00 31

POST

Letter boxes in France are yellow. Some have a separate slot for international mail (*étranger*).

Stamps are available at tobacconists and post offices. La Poste is the national post office. Main branch ✉ 1 boulevard Carnot ☎ 03 20 21 95 00 🕐 Mon–Fri 8–6.30, Sat 8–12. The post office at Euralille is open until 7pm Mon–Sat.

TIPS/GRATUITIES

Yes ✓ No ✗		
Hotels (service included)	✓	change
Restaurants (service included)	✓	change
Cafés (service included)	✓	change
Taxis	✓	€1/2
Tour guides	✓	€1/2
Porters	✓	€1/2
Usherettes	✓	€1
Hairdressers	✓	€1/2
Cloakroom attendants	✓	change
Toilets	✓	change

Acknowledgements

The Automobile Association would like to thank the following photographers and libraries for their assistance in the preparation of this book:

ALAMY 28; DIAF/H GYSSELS 21b; DIAPHOR 13b (© Bardoux), 17b (© JP Duplan), 23b (© P Mores), 33b (© M Langrand), 39 (© M Langrand), 41 (© Light Motiv); MARY EVANS PICTURE LIBRARY 10b; FRENCH PICTURE LIBRARY 6b, 16b, 22c, 29b; INTERNATIONAL PHOTOBANK 20b; MRI BANKERS' GUIDE TO FOREIGN CURRENCY 60; LAURENCE PHILLIPS 5a, 6a, 7a, 8, 9a, 10a, 11a, 12a, 13a, 14a, 15a, 16a, 17a, 18a, 19a, 20a, 21a, 22a, 23a, 24, 25, 26, 27a, 27b, 29a, 30a, 32a, 33a, 34a, 35a, 38a; PICTURES COLOUR LIBRARY 9b; REFLEXION 2, 5b, 7c, 7d, 12b, 15b, 15c, 18b, 22b, 30b, 31, 34b, 40, 47b, 59b (P Cheuva), 42, 45, (S Bellet); SPECTRUM COLOUR LIBRARY 11b, 19b, 32b, 35b, 36, 38b, 59a; WORLD PICTURES 1, 7b, 14b, 18/19

The remaining photographs are held in the Association's own library (AA PHOTOLIBRARY) and were taken by: P AITHIE 43, 44a, 44b, 45a, 46a; ROB MOORE 63a, 63b; DOUGLAS ROBERTSON 37, 46b; MICHAEL SHORT 47a, 48, 49, 50, 51, 52, 53, 54, 55, 56, 57, 58

The Atlas

Acknowledgements
All pictures are from AA World Travel Library with contributions from the following photographers:
Douglas Robertson: The church of St-Maurice, Grand' Place (place du Général du Gaulle),
La Préfecture
Roger Day: Cathédral Notre Dame de la Treille, regional specialties, boulangerie, café scene at
Grand' Place (place du Général du Gaulle)

www.theAA.com
The Automobile Association's website offers comprehensive and up-to-the-minute information covering AA-approved hotels, guest houses and B&Bs, restaurants and pubs in the UK; airport parking, insurance, European breakdown cover, European motoring advice, a ferry planner, European route planner, overseas fuel prices, a bookshop and much more.

www.aaa.com
AAA's website offers comprehensive information covering AAA-approved hotels and restaurants in the US. In addition, AAA can assist US citizens with obtaining a passport, reservations and tickets for cruise, tour, motorcoach, rail and air travel. AAA provides information on independent or escorted tours for individuals or groups and offers benefits on cruises, tours and travel packages.

The Foreign and Commonwealth Office
Country advice, traveller's tips, before you go information, checklists and more.
www.fco.gov.uk

French Government Tourist Office
Travel planner, how to get around, places of interest, festivals and events, shopping.
www.franceguide.com

GENERAL
UK Passport Service
www.ukpa.gov.uk

US Passport Information
www.travel.state.gov

Health Advice for Travellers
www.dh.gov.uk/traveladvice

BBC – Holiday
www.bbc.co.uk/holiday

The Full Universal Currency Converter
www.xe.com/ucc

Flying with Kids
Tips and advice for flying with babies and very young children
www.flyingwithkids.com

www.lilletourism.com
Lille tourist office online; ideal for checking updated opening hours.

www.transpole.fr
Useful route planner for the Greater Lille public transport system, with details of tickets and combined travel and museum passes.

www.lchti.com
Online reviews of nightlife and restaurants – as prepared by local students.

www.nord-gay.com
Listings of gay bars and clubs in Lille.

TRAVEL
Flights and Information
www.cheapflights.co.uk
www.thisistravel.co.uk
www.ba.com
www.continental.com
www.worldairportguide.com

Rail travel
www.raileurope.com
www.railbookers.com

Main road / Hauptstraße / Route principale

Other roads / Sonstige Straßen / Autres routes

Parking / Parkplatz /Parking

Underground / U-Bahn / Métro

Main railway with station / Hauptbahn mit Bahnhof /
Chemin de fer principal avec gare

Church / Kirche / Église

Public building / Öffentliches Gebäude / Bâtiment public

Gardens and parks / Gärten und Parks / Jardins et parcs

0		500 m
0		500 yards

Wambrechies

Bois
de la Deule

A

5

Pont du
Petit
Paradis

B

Allée des Marronniers

FAÇADE DE L'ESPLANADE

St-André

Rue Princesse

RUE ROYALE

Rue Saint-André

Rue Voltaire

Rue Négrier

Rue Jean M

C

Maison Na
du Géné
de Gau

Citadelle

Pont du
Ramponneau

R.Sainte-Catherine

Rue

4

Ave du 43ème Regt d'Infanterie

P

Ave Cuvier

R.Léonard Danel

Ste-Catherine

Bois de
Boulogne

Parc
Zoologique

Pont de
la Citadelle

Rue de la Barre

Quai du Wault

Rue de la Halloterie

Avenue Mathias Delobel

Avenue Léon Jouhaux

Jardin
Vauban

AVE LÉON
JOUHAUX

RUE DESMAZIÈRES

BOULEVARD VAUBAN

Square
Dutilleul

Rue de Tenremonde

Rue de l'Arc

square
Foch

BOULEVARD DE LA LIBERTÉ

RUE

P'tit Quinquin

3

Ave de l'Architecte
Louis Cordonnier

Rue de Calais

Rue de Toul

RUE DE SOLFÉRINO

Rue Patou

Rue de Bourgogne

Rue Jacquemars Giélée

de Puebla

Rue du Port

Square
Rameau

Rue Colson

Rue Boucher de Perthes

Rue Jean San

Sacré
Coeur

Rue du Faisan

R du Maire André

2

Rue Colbert

BOULEVARD VAUBAN

Rue du Port

RUE NATIONALE

Rue Meurein

Rue Meurein

Rue Alphonse Mercier

Les
Halles

Masséna

P

Rue

Place du
Maréchal
Leclerc

Rue des Stations

R Charles Quint

Rue de Ratisbonne

Rue Léon Gambetta

RUE DE SOLF

P

Théâtre
Sébastopol

Rue Henri Kolb

Place de
Sébastopol

Rue de

Mais
Coill

I

R Deschodt

Rue de la Tranquillité

Rue Léon Gambetta

Rue Colbert

Rue Dumerin

Marché de
Wazemmes

Place de la
Nouvelle Aventure

St-Pierre et
St-Paul

Rue du Marché

Rue Mourmant

Rue de Flandre

Rue Manuel

Gambetta

Rue Littré

R Louis Faure

Rue des postes

Rue Cantois

M

70

Rue des Croix des Sarrazins

A

B

C

Lille Street Index